Strengthening the Teaching Assistant Faculty

John D. W. Andrews, *Editor*

NEW DIRECTIONS FOR TEACHING AND LEARNING
KENNETH E. EBLE, *Editor-in-Chief*

Number 22, June 1985

Paperback sourcebooks in
The Jossey-Bass Higher Education Series

Jossey-Bass Inc., Publishers
San Francisco • Washington • London

John D. W. Andrews (Ed.).
Strengthening the Teaching Assistant Faculty.
New Directions for Teaching and Learning, no. 22.
San Francisco: Jossey-Bass, 1985.

New Directions for Teaching and Learning Series
Kenneth E. Eble, *Editor-in-Chief*

New Directions for Teaching and Learning is published quarterly
by Jossey-Bass Inc., Publishers. Subscriptions, single-issue
orders, change of address notices, undelivered copies, and other
correspondence should be sent to Subscriptions, Jossey-Bass Inc.,
Publishers, 433 California Street, San Francisco, California 94104.

Editorial correspondence should be sent to the Editor-in-Chief,
Kenneth E. Eble, Department of English, University of Utah,
Salt Lake City, Utah 84112.

Library of Congress Catalogue Card Number LC 84-82381

International Standard Serial Number ISSN 0271-0633

International Standard Book Number ISBN 87589-772-X

Cover art by Willi Baum

Manufactured in the United States of America

Ordering Information

The paperback sourcebooks listed below are published quarterly and can be ordered either by subscription or single-copy.

Subscriptions cost $35.00 per year for institutions, agencies, and libraries. Individuals can subscribe at the special rate of $25.00 per year *if payment is by personal check.* (Note that the full rate of $35.00 applies if payment is by institutional check, even if the subscription is designated for an individual.) Standing orders are accepted. Subscriptions normally begin with the first of the four sourcebooks in the current publication year of the series. When ordering, please indicate if you prefer your subscription to begin with the first issue of the *coming* year.

Single copies are available at $8.95 when payment accompanies order, and *all single-copy orders under $25.00 must include payment.* (California, New Jersey, New York, and Washington, D.C., residents please include appropriate sales tax.) For billed orders, cost per copy is $8.95 plus postage and handling. (Prices subject to change without notice.)

Bulk orders (ten or more copies) of any individual sourcebook are available at the following discounted prices: 10–49 copies, $8.05 each; 50–100 copies, $7.15 each; over 100 copies, *inquire.* Sales tax and postage and handling charges apply as for single copy orders.

To ensure correct and prompt delivery, all orders must give either the *name of an individual* or an *official purchase order number.* Please submit your order as follows:

Subscriptions: specify series and year subscription is to begin.
Single Copies: specify sourcebook code (such as, TL8) and first two words
of title.

Mail orders for United States and Possessions, Latin America, Canada, Japan, Australia, and New Zealand to:
Jossey-Bass Inc., Publishers
433 California Street
San Francisco, California 94104

Mail orders for all other parts of the world to:
Jossey-Bass Limited
28 Banner Street
London EC1Y 8QE

New Directions for Teaching and Learning Series
Kenneth E. Eble, *Editor-in-Chief*

Contents

Editor's Notes

The role of teaching assistant (TA) is one of the most creative inventions in the hsitory of higher education. This statement may sound strange, because the TA is a familiar and ordinary part of the landscape, and the role is not usually thought of as having been invented. If the role did not exist, however, its invention would be a creative solution to a number of important problems.

The TA role provides a source of financial support to graduate students. It greatly eases the institutional problem of a high student-faculty ratio, thereby improving the opportunities for teacher-student contact. And it does so at a reasonable cost. Also, by generating a corps of teachers intermediate between faculty and undergraduates in terms of age and experience, it provides peer communication and empathy for student learning problems. The TA role is the basis of an apprenticeship system that enables graduate students to learn teaching skills through modeling and practice and to ease gradually into the role of professor. An important element in this experience is that graduate students—in keeping with the adage that "the best way to learn something is to try to teach it"—have the opportunity to consolidate their basic knowledge and replace the passive stance in which it may have been learned originally with an active mastery evoked by teaching.

Many of these advantages are well summed up by Pickering (1983): "It is of course true that professors do teach, if by teach you mean standing in front of a lecture hall of hundreds of students and broadcasting information. But if one thinks of teaching as an intimate two-way process of dialogue, of criticism, of honing one mind with another, then most of it is done by TA's. For it is they who are charged with answering questions (so they play the part of Socrates in the dialogue)." The function of developing critical minds is generally seen as a crucial one in higher education, as a glance at almost any college catalogue will show. In most universities, TAs make the accomplishment of this vitally important goal possible. This is a great responsibility, and it places an equally significant responsibility on those who are charged with training and supervising TAs.

Of course, there is a large measure of illogic and expediency in placing this most vital educational goal in the hands of the least qualified and experienced corps of teachers. On research-oriented campuses, the demands of scholarship and graduate courses mean that teaching is not the most important of priorities. Thus, people with no interest in teaching are thrust into the classroom; TAs feel exploited by doing a demanding job for a low wage; and individuals who were selected solely on the basis of intellectual skill are nevertheless asked to learn how to teach. Moreover, the utilitarian aspects of the TA role lead faculty and TAs alike to overlook the apprenticeship opportunity, so

1

that minimal TA training is provided. Often, too, when the teaching function is taken for granted in this way, the need of TAs for a well-defined job description is overlooked, at a time when their concept of that job is most unformed. TAs are called on to exert or represent educational authority, especially in grading, but their age and status work against this role. Furthermore, the student habits of graduate students often die hard; when they become teachers, they may continue to think in terms of demonstrating their own knowledge rather than helping others to acquire it, and this stance interferes with effective instruction.

This enumeration of difficulties may seem to show that, far from being a creative solution to problems, the TA role itself creates problems and cross-purposes. Both perspectives are correct, and to have an effective TA staff, an institution must maximize the benefits and cope with the liabilities. A campus-wide TA development program can accomplish this goal, so that the various functions of the TA role can be made to reinforce one another, rather than being allowed to interfere with each other. Adopting and implementing this goal is the most valuable contribution that can be made by those responsible for TA development at the campuswide level.

A complete TA development program must deal with the fact that TAs are experiencing several kinds of transitions simultaneously. They are learning to deal with institutional reward systems that affect the distribution of effort and time. They are moving from being recent graduates, concerned with orientation to new departments and campuses, through a process of professional socialization and then departure for the job market. Identity formation is also occurring; the student is developing career goals and making the transition from consumer of knowledge to producer and transmitter. This involves testing and refining new abilities and elaborating one's personal work identity (Erikson, 1969). TAs also are learning to be teachers, discovering the extent of their teaching aptitudes in spheres they may not even have considered in making their graduate school plans. This process includes adapting to the specific role of TA and learning the part one plays as a TA in university education as a whole.

Taking responsibility for this broader process involves looking at the entire career of a TA, beginning with entry into graduate school and ending with departure and readiness for full professional responsibility. At many points in this process, we must ask how the institutional structure impinges on the graduate student's development as a teacher and how these factors can be made to reinforce each other positively. This approach deals with a number of issues not ordinarily included in TA training. Here are some examples.

Department A found through TA feedback (collected with the help of the campus TA program) that the logistics of arranging the first TA assignment were having a negative impact on teaching. Assignments were made at the last minute, and the TA's knowledge and interests were rarely taken into account. As a result, TAs spent most of the term running to catch up on course material. They had little time to think about teaching approaches. Moreover, they also absorbed a general atmosphere that made teaching concerns a low priority. By providing advance information, soliciting data on teaching preferences, and including graduate students in the TA assignment committee, Department A rearranged the context of TA work and significantly improved the climate in which TA training activities were conducted.

In Department B, it was realized that the supervisory relationship between professors and TAs was not working. With the help of the campus TA development program, several structural changes were made. The graduate adviser held meetings to spell out expectations for the TA role. The end-of-term formal evaluation provided by the faculty member was revamped and implemented more consistently. An award for excellence in teaching was instituted, and future TA assignments were made contingent on acceptable performance. TAs with serious teaching problems were referred to the TA development program for special consultation. The outcome was that TAs and faculty began to view the TA role more seriously, and — as in Department A — TA attitudes toward training workshops improved.

Department C was concerned about the role of TA work in its graduate students' career plans. Jointly with the campus TA development program, it conducted a survey of campuses that had advertised job openings. It was found that teaching skill, with a weighting of 42 percent over all the 60 campuses responding, played a significant role in hiring criteria, and that certain ways of documenting teaching competence were particularly credible; a sample teaching session on the hiring campus was most favored. This information was publicized, which helped graduate students focus their teaching concerns and their job-seeking efforts. Department C and the TA development program instituted supporting activities, including a teaching portfolio service, which would help TAs compile data on their teaching from the start (instead of at the last moment), and the opportunity to practice sample teaching sessions through videotape feedback. These activities helped TAs think about the role of teaching in their career goals and built the teaching apprenticeship more strongly into the entire graduate career.

On the University of California at San Diego campus, we have systematized our attention to these concerns via a questionnaire, administered to all TAs, which explores the climate for teaching in their departments and the specific factors that influence it. Regarding TA assignments, for example, we ask for several ratings, such as the extent to which the TA selection process is clear and well organized, with adequate lead-time. We also explore the TA-professor relationship, asking, for example, whether the instructor sets a tone of concern for good teaching or handles the official end-of-quarter written evaluation in a constructive, informative way. Many other aspects of the teaching apprenticeship are examined in a similar fashion. Thus, we gain a diagnosis of how departmental structure impinges on TAs' experience and opportunities to develop teaching skill, and we pinpoint what most important changes should be made.

This volume is designed to explore all the ramifications of TA development programming as sketched above. This is a wider perspective than has usually been adopted in the past. An examination of the published literature on TA training shows that the almost exclusive focus has been on describing or evaluating designs for training programs themselves (Carroll, 1980). This is a reasonable place to start, but we are likely to develop viable training systems only if we also address contextual forces that affect the shape and, often, the survival of such systems. Bergquist and Phillips (1975) propose that any improvement program must address instructional development, personal development, and organizational development. This volume touches on all three areas.

Chapter One, by Boehrer and Sarkisian, presents the viewpoints of TAs themselves, showing how they experience the various forces that shape the teaching apprenticeship and exploring the subjective meaning that teaching can take on in relation to the personal goals of each TA. The teaching responsibility, and the rewards and disappointments that flow from it, importantly shape graduate students' feelings about themselves. The resulting changes in self-image also affect future expectations and career plans.

Chapter Two, by Smock and Menges, delineates some alternatives for situating TA development programs within the institutional structure of a campus. These authors spell out different patterns currently in use, describe the advantages and disadvantages of each, and suggest certain combinations that they believe to be most fruitful.

Chapter Three, by Wilson and Stearns, examines the TA-professor relationship and the work setting of the TA role in undergraduate courses. These authors describe various theories of how the TA role should be structured, and present a case example showing how organizational-change methods can be used to enhance the instructional and apprenticeship functions of the role.

Chapter Four, by Andrews, examines the TA job itself and proposes three core functions that seem to be universals of the role. The chapter goes on to emphasize the distinctive nature of the TA role as different from, but complementary to, the professorial role. This chapter also describes a planning guide to help TAs understand the unique requirements of teaching any given course and suggests some innovative teaching formats to help TAs do their jobs in more effective and exciting ways.

Chapter Five, by Fisher, draws on the varied perspectives discussed earlier to examine the "foreign TA problem." As the numbers of foreign graduate students increase and they are more often placed in direct-contact TA roles, the question of their readiness to teach American undergraduates has become important. Fisher discusses this issue in terms of institutional policies; training program designs; teaching skills; the subjective experiences of foreign TAs; and the role of supervising faculty in helping these individuals adapt to the teaching role as defined in American higher education.

Finally, in Chapter Six, the contributors to this volume have traced a theme that runs through all the preceding chapters: how to set up and nurture TA development programs. The services we deliver and the concepts we disseminate are closely intertwined with the process of ensuring that TA training will take root strongly within the institution. We stress that this process must involve building a network of support throughout the university, a network based on careful identification of needs to be filled and problems to be solved. Fostering this sort of collaborative spirit is an additional benefit that a TA development program can bring to the campus.

John D. W. Andrews
Editor

References

Bergquist, W. H., and Phillips, S. R. "Components of an Effective Faculty Development Program." *Journal of Higher Education*, 1975, *46*, 177–212.

Carroll, J. G. "Effects of Training Programs for University Teaching Assistants." *Journal of Higher Education*, 1980, *51* (2), 167–183.

Erikson, E. H. "The Problem of Ego Identity." In M. R. Stein, A. J. Vidich, and D. M. White (Eds.), *Identity and Anxiety*. Glencoe, Ill.: The Free Press, 1969.

Pickering, M. "Should Teaching Assistants Be Asked to Play the Part of Socrates?" *Chronicle of Higher Education*, June 29, 1983, p. 56.

John D. W. Andrews is director of teaching development programs at the University of California, San Diego. He is also a clinical psychologist with Student Psychological Services.

Teaching assistants' viewpoints powerfully condition not only how they will teach but also how they will respond to programs for developing teaching skills.

The Teaching Assistant's Point of View

John Boehrer
Ellen Sarkisian

In the view of some graduate students, the job of TA is the apprenticeship to a lifelong career. For others, it is simply a convenient way for the university to disburse financial aid. This contrast illustrates the variety of ways in which TAs view the job. More important, it underlines the fact that for each graduate student who adds the responsibility of teaching to the challenge of graduate study, the job is an individual experience. TAs decide for themselves what importance and meaning it has, and in doing the job, they strive for effectiveness when they find it personally meaningful to do so. If they realize their potential as teachers, it is by expressing their individuality in the TA role.

Deans, professors, department heads, teaching consultants — those who would help TAs increase their effectiveness — need to recognize TAs' points of view and respond to their individual experiences. They need to provide TAs help that both supports learning and fosters the development of each one's own teaching voice. For the most part, when they begin, TAs do not know how to teach. They need help, but they do not want or need just to be told how to do it. Learning to teach is, after all, like learning anything else: less a matter of accumulating information than of acquiring skills and solving problems in pursuit of some personal goal. The challenge for anyone who would help TAs

J. D. W. Andrews (Ed.). *Strengthening the Teaching Assistant Faculty.* New Directions for Teaching and Learning, no. 22. San Francisco: Jossey-Bass, June 1985.

is to make effectiveness rewarding and possible by helping them learn and develop through teaching itself, rather than attempting to impose some paradigm of good teaching on them.

In this chapter we begin by considering the TA's view of the job, what is typical of that view, and what different kinds of meaning TAs tend to find in the experience. Next, we explore the TA's interaction with the institution and the students involved. Finally, we turn to the experience of teaching itself, the ways that teaching assistants develop in the job, and the use they can make of any help they receive in that development. In examining their perspectives, we devote attention to several issues that confront TAs as they make the transition from graduate student to teacher. Among these are the adequacy of their knowledge and teaching skills, their exercise of authority over others, their responsibility for the learning of others, the stress of critical self-evaluation, the isolation that characterizes their experience, and the challenge of developing their own teaching voices.

The illustrations we use come from conversations with graduate students, both in consultations with them about their teaching at Harvard and in separate interviews with TAs from other institutions. We refer several times to the words and experiences of three individuals, whom we call Kevin, Cynthia, and Rachel. All three were very thoughtful about teaching, but their experiences of the role were different, and they varied in their enjoyment of it. Kevin, who always assumed he would be a teacher, took to the role with relative ease. Rachel had more success with teaching than she had anticipated, but confirmed her expectation that she would not like teaching or want to pursue it. Cynthia, who expected to teach only while she was in graduate school, took great satisfaction in making science accessible to her students.

The Individual Point of View

The individual point of view originates in each TA's personal background. Previous schooling (often at institutions unlike the ones where they are doing graduate work), perceptions of role models (which they shun as often as emulate), and expectations about their own teaching all influence TAs' experiences of the job. Individual perspectives are strongly determined by the reasons for coming to graduate school in the first place: A graduate student may focus primarily on studying psychology, with the expectation of going on to combine research with teaching at a university (as Kevin did), or social science, with an eye toward a role in public policy (as Rachel did), or geology, in hopes of working for a mining company (the course that Cynthia pursued). Katz and Hartnett (1976) found that more students went to graduate school to pursue an interest in a subject than to carry out career intentions. They also found that most graduate students (85 percent in biochemistry and psychology; nearly all in English) expected to teach some time after leaving graduate school. In any case, graduate study is the central activity of TAs at the university. Even the most dedicated TAs, in their own eyes, are graduate students absorbed in completing course work, passing generals, or writing theses.

Significance Attached to the Job. Whether the TA views the job as the first step toward a professional vocation or as source of subsistence, teaching is inescapably a significant responsibility that challenges one's sense of adequacy. Many TAs anticipate the semester with panic, wondering if they know enough to teach. When they actually start teaching, their doubts may grow as they realize that students are treating them as authorities. Uncertainty manifests itself in persistent questions: What am I supposed to be doing? Am I doing it right?

Whatever previous tasks TAs have undertaken, including caring for others, they probably have been responsible primarily for their own performance. As TAs, they take some responsibility for the performance of others in complex and difficult intellectual endeavors. It is a thoroughly adult role, very often the first one the graduate student has taken on. While Kevin welcomed teaching his first psychology section as "a real opportunity, since it was a small piece of the course that was mine," another TA, who had complete charge of a seminar, said, "Those who are on their own feel responsible for getting students fascinated with the material."

In several facets of their role, TAs are highly exposed. They are delegates of authority and instruction for the institution, surrogates for the faculty (whom students sometimes find inaccessible), and leaders in the pursuit of knowledge (and good grades) for students. It is small wonder, then, than graduate students who are comfortable writing about the subtleties of Shakespeare or experimenting with particle physics may shudder upon walking in to teach a class. Speaking in front of a group, which most people find frightening, is just one of their routine activities. Worse still, as one put it, they are frequently teaching "at the limits of our knowledge." They often must deal with material outside their own specialties—material that, along with their students, they have just encountered in the previous week's lecture. Teaching also demands energy, attention, and time. One of the most frequent complaints among TAs is that no one told them how much time teaching would take. It may be just a job, but it is not the same straightforward economic exchange as alphabetizing a card catalogue for the library or operating a slide projector for the fine arts department.

Impact of the Job. Even when it is not an intended career direction, teaching rivals graduate study as an influence on self-esteem. Although graduate students may regard teaching as a subordinate activity, it is difficult to escape the outlook that graduate study is still preparation, while teaching is actual performance, and the quality of his or her performance is likely to register strongly on the individual. Distress and exhilaration are more common than indifference.

Many graduate students have high ideals about teaching, as well as high expectations of themselves as teachers. In the opinion of a junior professor who works with many TAs in her own undergraduate course, they are the people in her university who care most about teaching. Their desire to do well at what they have spent years criticizing others for doing poorly can be intense, and doing it well can have a powerful impact on them. Cynthia, for example, talked about how she loved to see the light of understanding come into her students' faces. Kevin said that just having an audience to talk to about his field of interest was like hearing applause. He added, "If you do in fact impart any learning to them, then you have affected their lives forever."

Discouragement can just as easily result, although its sources are more bewildering. Self-doubt can arise from struggling to get students to participate in discussion, from seeing them perform poorly on an examination, or from watching attendance dwindle as the semester drags on. Perhaps the worst aspect of such discouragement is that it is often endured alone. The guilt Rachel felt for having reprimanded a student in her first class plagued her until the end of the semester, when a chance conversation with the professor in the course persuaded her that she was incapable of doing the harm for which she had been blaming herself. Rachel said, "You can really carry with you this whole burden of what terrible things you're doing to a student."

Inadequate performance rarely causes a graduate student to lose a teaching assistantship, but self-censure for doing a poor job can be severe; those who excel academically typically possess high expectations of themselves. Similarly, although rewards for excellence are only slightly more common than penalties for inadequacy, personal satisfaction derived from one's own good teaching is also significant; some TAs develop entirely new career intentions because of it. A former TA, now an assistant professor of history, said that since only a few graduate students were selected to teach in her department, those who did felt "anointed." That perspective shaped her expectations, and through the experience she discovered her love of teaching. Cynthia, who thoroughly enjoyed her teaching assistantship in geology, now plans to spend several peripatetic years in mining exploration and then return to teaching as a means of achieving the stability necessary to raise a family. Although such experiences are not uncommon, the TA job is less often a turning point on the graduate student's career path than it is an opportunity to discover and test personal qualities and develop a repertoire of skills that may be relevant to many intended professions. In carrying out their responsibilities, TAs typically reveal that, however they regard the job, the experience is seldom devoid of personal meaning, and it is frequently the stimulus for some important self-discovery.

Interacting with the Institution. Some graduate students regard the teaching assistantship itself as evidence of institutional ambivalence toward teaching. They point out that while TAs make better teacher-student ratios possible, they also give faculty more time for research. The importance of research, and of their own graduate work in particular, looms large for TAs. Inevitably, the focus on research influences their efforts to be effective, and sometimes even undermines effectiveness. Subtly or directly, TAs often receive the message that teaching is not the top priority. A dean at a western university tells beginning teachers, TAs and faculty alike, "Aim for a B in teaching. Get your research started. Understand the rules of the game. You can work on teaching later."

Course heads and academic departments communicate their attitudes toward teaching through their hiring practices. Even within a single department, attitudes can vary between the almost casual assignment of teaching duties in the process of awarding financial aid and the most careful, competitive selection procedure. Whatever the process, it colors the TA's whole experience of the job.

A political science professor at one university personally interviews graduate students from throughout his institution to select only those TAs who meet his standards. As a result, they feel they are part of an elite group. They are informed about the professor's goals, and they have access to him when questions come up in their teaching. In contrast, Kevin reported that he learned of his teaching assistantship in psychology by receiving a letter and a reading list from his department. When he arrived in the fall to begin teaching, the course head and the senior TA were away at a conference. He had to greet his students on the first day of class without any additional guidance about the course.

Timing alone can contribute significantly to the impact of the hiring experience. One TA complained that his department did not assign him to teach a seminar until after the term had begun, even though the students had registered for the course the previous semester. He was demoralized about teaching and felt that he could have done a much better job had his department given him time to prepare. In contrast, another TA in the same university felt that she taught effectively in her first semester because she had met all the students the previous spring and designed learning activities according to their particular backgrounds and interests. She was excited about continuing to sharpen her ability to tailor her teaching to the students' intellectual abilities.

Often it is apparent to TAs that there is only a tenuous relationship between aptitude for teaching and teaching assignments. More often, availability, eligibility for financial aid, familiarity with the course staff, and past performance as a student are the most prominent factors in matching TAs with courses. Only rarely does a course head have the time, inclination, and number of applicants to consider their individual suitability for teaching, although some do recognize that the TA selection process is the last chance for quality control.

Hiring without much concern for teaching ability places a burden on the more competent TAs. Kevin complained that he should have been assigned both sections in an introductory course his second year. "Someone else needed the money and got the job. I ended up doing her work and not being paid. It's not fair to the students, the professor, or the other TAs to give someone a job based on need. If graduate students are not capable of teaching, the university should find another way to disburse financial aid."

One course head who relied on good hiring to ensure good teaching confessed to being "frankly puzzled" about whether to provide teacher training activities. Such activities might divert energy and attention away from research. Further, the distance many professors keep from their teaching assistants' work reveals an uncertainty about how best to give guidance. Experienced teachers and administrators know that beginning teachers need the freedom to take personal positions on the issues teaching raises for everyone. The question is always this: How much neglect is truly benign? Rachel recalled being aware of her course head's dilemma. She said, "Even the professor who was trying his best to give us what we wanted couldn't quite decide what we should get." At the same time, she and her fellow TAs still wanted the guidance. Their constant question was: "Why aren't they giving us more?"

While some professors hesitate to interfere with their TAs' work, others give it considerable attention. Individual course heads sometimes issue written guides to their TAs or visit their classes. Regular staff meetings take place within many courses. Some deans offer incentives to generate discussions of teaching within departments, and departments themselves often conduct teacher orientation and training sessions at the start of the semester. The impact of these efforts on actual teaching effectiveness is difficult to assess, but the more specifically they apply to immediate experience, the more useful they are likely to be. A course head who gives graduate credit to TAs for participating in weekly training and discussion sessions emphasized that instructional development must be offered within the context of actual teaching because people do not like to read about or discuss teaching in the abstract. Her meetings provide an opportunity to talk about classroom experiences that participants are actually having.

The major benefit of many of these attempts to focus on teaching may be the sense of concern they convey. The professor's presence in the classroom can make a TA nervous, but most appreciate the attention. One who had been feeling worried and inadequate about dealing with some particularly difficult students was relieved by her professor's understanding words: "Now I know what you're up against."

Despite these signals of genuine concern, TAs routinely report that they receive little or no guidance either before they begin teaching or while they teach. One said she simply felt abandoned: "I was thrown into teaching. I didn't know what I was doing and I still don't. How can I, when I don't get any feedback?" In fact, the question of their effectiveness often remains uncomfortably open for TAs. End-of-course evaluations may offer some indication of performance, but during the semester, when feedback would contribute directly to their teaching — and to their self-esteem — it is typically unavailable. "We can afford to be really irresponsible with our teaching," one concerned TA pointed out to a group of his peers. "What difference does it make? No one is evaluating us. No one tells us how we're doing."

A casual observer might expect overworked graduate students to appreciate such loose supervision, but TAs also can understand it to mean that, from the institution's point of view, their teaching is not important, and that perception can be discouraging. Clearly, an institution — through its stated policies, public pronouncements, and actions of administrators and faculty — has an obligation both to acknowledge the importance of the TA's work and to provide guidance in developing strengths and correcting weaknesses.

Interacting with Students. In contrast to the intense, private intellectual pressures of thesis writing that preoccupy many graduate students, classroom teaching offers the possibility of lively interaction with students. Nevertheless, the classroom also presents complexities that can be as demanding to resolve as a thesis is to write. One usually becomes a graduate student, and a TA, by being good at a subject. That achievement can result from hard work, but aptitude for learning almost always accompanies the effort. Watching students ponder what appears easy to grasp, TAs discover that students' learning does not necessarily mirror their own, either in extent or in style. When he began to teach, Kevin was surprised to find that he overprepared for class. "Since I had just read for the first time the same material they had for homework, it was hard for me to think that I should teach it to them. We both had the same book. It seemed presumptuous to assume I understood it better." Yet he soon realized that he did not have to think up new insights for each week's class; his students were still trying to understand the material at a more fundamental level.

A still more disquieting discovery is the fact that teaching a class is much more complex than tutoring an individual. Inexperienced TAs frequently report that they can help a student who comes individually, but they feel lost in front of a class. The problem is partly that, while they interact naturally with other individuals, most TAs have to learn how to interpret and respond to the feedback they get from a group. In addition, few TAs will have classes in which the variety among students themselves is not a constant problem.

In his study of undergraduates at Harvard, Perry (1968) saw that the intellectual development of college students ranges from the early insistence that to all questions there are right answers (which they expect the teacher to know), through the later recognition of diverse opinion and the acceptance of reasonable disagreement, to the mature stage of commitment to ideas generated from one's own thinking and values. Since college students represent the whole range, it is necessary for a TA to be prepared to cope with a bewildering mixture of student expectations.

TAs have to press students to think independently because, as Perry points out, students tend to associate authority with textbooks and teachers. Many graduate students have exercised authority in such earlier contexts as camp counseling or student government. When they become TAs, however, they suddenly acquire authority far more extensive and less defined than what most of them have yet encountered, and they have to figure out what to do with it. Speaking about the experiences of new TAs, Rachel said, "When we're beginning to confront what's expected of us, authority hits us so clearly. It's one of the things we have to decide for ourselves; what it means and how to use it."

The TA role requires one to choose among many possible stances on issues that range from discipline to grading. TAs have to decide how forcefully to maintain order in the classroom, how closely to monitor assignments, how persuasively to advocate their views of a subject, how deliberately to act as role models, how profoundly to influence their students' views of their own capabilities and aspirations, and how rigorously to evaluate student work. They must even decide, sometimes, how deeply to get involved in their students' personal lives.

The stances that an individual takes are personal, and the sense of authority they reveal can vary considerably with the issue. An undergraduate in a sociology course asked his TA to pester him about his term paper so that he would hand it in on time. She declined, telling him he would have to take responsibility for doing his own work. Relating the incident later, she recalled, "I just didn't want to be his mother." In conducting her classes, she attempted to foster her students' intellectual autonomy as well and often gave them the task of leading entire discussions. At the same time, she counseled her peers to be active in encouraging gifted students to pursue advanced study. "I don't know about the rest of you," she said, "but I know I wouldn't have considered graduate school if someone hadn't taken me aside and suggested that I had the ability to go on."

TAs' decisions about authority often involve considerations of how justified they feel in exercising it and how readily their students will respond. During an orientation session, TAs in a biology course listened to a senior professor's admonition to urge students to think (Westheimer, 1982). He said, "One has to ask students in laboratory again and again what it is they are trying to do and question them, not tell them what they're doing. Make them tell you." After hearing this, an inexperienced teaching assistant agreed with the reasoning of his approach, but she also expressed her nervousness about asking students to tell her what they were doing. "What if they don't answer?" she wondered.

Of all the requirements to exercise authority, evaluating student work is the most daunting. When asked about her first experience grading examinations, one TA in political science recalled, "It was awful, for three reasons. The first was a question of competence. Did I know enough to be an authority? The second reason was that I felt I was responsible for all the blanks and bored handwriting in the blue books. Third, I didn't have any standards. An A really stands out, but I couldn't tell an A – from a B + ."

A colleague in social studies concurred. "I was so afraid of being arbitrary." he said. "The first time I marked exams, it took so long! I put them in piles, and I kept revising the rank-ordering. I longed for an absolute standard that didn't exist." He went on to say, "The most unpleasant part of teaching is having students come to challenge a grade. Not being confident enough to stand by the grade, a TA is really caught. I sat there for three hours the first time arguing."

Subjective judgment, which plagues TAs in grading students, is still virtually all they have to rely on in their efforts to determine how effective their teaching is. In the absence of clear criteria, any reaction to their performance makes a powerful impression. One beginning TA felt severely demoralized when some disgruntled students walked out of his third economics class. He was elated at the end of the course, however, when those who had stayed gave him high ratings. "That was the real reward," he said, "for all my hard work — far beyond the small amount of money I was paid."

As reassuring as they may be, student evaluations of teaching are often inconsistent and difficult to interpret, since individual students react so differently to the same teaching effort and express themselves in judgmental rather than informative terms. This inconsistency, coupled with lack of clear guidance and supervision, makes it difficult for TAs to know how they are doing. The resulting need to generate and satisfy their own criteria of effectiveness is a major source of stress. A former chief of psychiatry at a university health service, reflecting on this uncertainty in the TA's experience, said, "It is impossible to succeed using conventional terms. You must move your source of self-esteem to within. When you teach, your self-esteem takes a beating like nowhere else" (Walters, 1982).

The Experience of Teaching

Assumed Competence. Within many academic departments, acceptance into a graduate program conveys an automatic license to teach. The extrapolation from academic to teaching ability does not apply only to graduate students, of course; college and university instructors, lecturers, and professors at all levels get their positions by proving research ability, not by preparing to teach. Unlike doctors and many other professionals, most college teachers practice on their clients without benefit of formal training. Almost inevitably, TAs adopt the prevailing view: If one can learn the subject, one can surely teach it. For the newly appointed TA, possibly the most immediate threat to self-esteem comes from the discrepancy between this assumption that one knows how to teach and the discovery that one does not.

Rachel reported that during her second semester as a TA in political science, she felt frustrated by well-intentioned advice from her colleagues about what she should have been doing to create productive discussion among her students. The advice described the desired result, but left out how to obtain it. She held her hands apart to illustrate the gap and said, "That's right where I need the help. I'm supposed to be able to get from here to there, but I don't know how to do that."

Knowing and Telling. A common corollary of the assumption that teaching ability flows automatically from successful study is the view, prevalent in many universities and shared by many TAs, that teaching is simply telling others what one knows. This view breeds expectations of knowing all the answers and fears of being caught without them. Graduate students approaching a first semester as TAs regularly anticipate, with anguish, the question they cannot answer. With experience, they begin to realize that teaching is something more than telling, that knowledge is necessary but not sufficient, and that it is more important to encourage students' learning than to display their own.

In the very telling of what they do know, TAs often discover that knowing something does not guarantee that they can teach it. Neither is communicating one's understanding of that idea to a patient teacher — as TAs have done in the role of student — the same as leading a willing student to a new understanding. Kevin said that what he learned from teaching was very simple: "You must decide what you want students to know, and then construct sentences in the right order to convey that knowledge. It takes a lot of work to find the best way to present a topic. Writing papers is not the same thing. Your audience is different. When you write, you are writing for someone who already knows."

In fact, telling what one knows can be complicated by the knowledge itself. Having advanced to graduate study themselves, TAs sometimes mix the essential with the esoteric or tell everything they know, to avoid what they regard as a misleading oversimplification. According to a TA in physics, "Many graduate students suffer from a misplaced idealism that they must be true to their subject in its purest form. It is easy to go over the undergraduate's heads." Because TAs typically teach in lower-level courses, they may also be bored. Both the oversophistication and the boredom result from focusing on the subject matter instead of engaging oneself with the students' own struggle to master the material.

The Teaching Role. The principal irony of the TA's situation is that of occupying the teaching role because of having been a successful student. Teaching, however, depends not just on one's own ability to learn, but also on such skills as diagnosing others' thought processes, skills that have little apparent connection with gaining entrance to graduate school. The essence of teaching is to facilitate rather than display learning.

Facilitating learning implies interpreting students' questions and comments. The TA's instinct may be simply to respond on cue, to answer the question or reply to the comment. That may be the appropriate action, but what students say also leads back to their thinking and presents an opportunity to find out what guidance or challenge they need. A TA in psychology who watched a videotape of her own teaching reflected that while her students talked she was preoccupied with what she might say next and was inattentive to indications of reasoning, interest, learning, or confusion coming from them. She traced her preoccupation to being a graduate student: "If I'm walking through my department and I run into someone who mentions a theory or the latest experiment, I'm supposed to have something to say about that." Upon deeper reflection, she said that her teaching role called for something different: listening to her students and being concerned with what was going on in their minds.

In interpreting what students say, TAs are likely to teach to the students that they themselves once were. For TAs to retrace their own steps does focus needed attention on students' learning, yet TAs are often unaware that focusing on their own learning styles results in communicating with only part of the class. Some of the students may indeed be on the same path to advanced study the TA has taken, but others have less aptitude, interest, confidence, or preparation and little intention of pursuing the subject beyond the basic level. Cynthia deliberately pitched her teaching of geology to the students who had always found science most intimidating; she demystified it by relating it to their familiar surroundings and took great pleasure in their growing confidence. That kind of appeal to students' learning processes requires an appreciation for experiences unlike one's own and a willingness to learn how to unlock knowledge for others.

Responsibility for Student Learning. A professor of education, whose own teaching is very well received, posed the central dilemma of teaching: "You cannot learn for someone else." As TAs, graduate students can confidently use their abilities to master a subject in preparing for teaching a class. Depending on their talents and perceptions, they can develop presentation and discussion-leading skills that offer their students good access to knowledge and understanding. Unlike graduate study, however, teaching presents TAs with the unnerving fact that, whatever their efforts, students' learning is beyond their immediate control. Pressure of responsibility for an outcome they cannot control, together with uncertainty about how to teach, can cause TAs significant anxiety. Often, TAs respond by maintaining whatever control they can. One strategy is clinging to the known role of student. Any number of TAs are their own best students, showing up their classes with superior answers and sophisticated points. A TA in history persistently corrected small errors in her students' comments, which she detected with ease. In doing so, she inhibited participation when she might have focused instead on the more appropriate task of understanding her students' remarks and building discussion. "The first principle of teaching," according to Fairbank (1982), "is to get on the same level of enterprise with the people you're talking to. . . . Don't tell them so much as question them."

Discussion typically confronts TAs with the difficult choice of taking over the conversation themselves or allowing students to grope. A TA in a literature course discovered that when he tried to generate discussion with an open question, he was confounded by his students' unrelated responses. To avoid this kind of discomfort, TAs often adopt such strategies as talking much more than listening, dispensing answers instead of proposing questions, drawing conclusions rather than letting students reach them, or simply lecturing.

Reflecting on why she stood at the head of her class dispensing information when what she wanted was to engage her students in discussion, Rachel acknowledged that her need to exercise control came from fears that her attempts to lead a discussion would result in a chaotic, insubstantial conversation. She allowed that she might sit down and talk with her students — the advice she was being offered — if she thought it would work, but she said she did not see how she could get them to talk purposefully about broad questions of political and social history.

The class that Rachel was reviewing on videotape with a teaching consultant had been about the labor movements in several European countries. When the teaching consultant suggested that she imagine what questions she might actually ask her students, she finally focused on the knowledge she personally had to offer on the subject; information about working-class life in those countries. She realized that it would be productive and interesting to ask her students to think about how the contrasts in daily living from country to country contributed to the differences among the labor movements that grew up. She also discovered that she was now imagining an actual discussion, one that would give expression to her genuine interests and allow students, with her guidance, to work toward conclusions. She left the consulting session excited about trying out her ideas.

The Individual's Own Voice. Some TAs try at first to teach like professors they have admired; others respond fitfully to the varied influences of students and other TAs. With experience, they learn to perform the role in an individual voice, to speak from a position of personal autonomy and express an authenthic personality in teaching. As they decide how to exercise authority and gain confidence interacting with students, they begin to relax. When newly acquired teaching skills become part of the TA's repertoire and no longer seem artificial, teaching grows more spontaneous (Kasulis, 1982). The TA matures in the job, the initial question of adequacy gives way to a concern with the accuracy of content and then to an interest in how well the students understand. When the TA begins to experience being competent in these ways, the central question can resolve itself into new questions about oneself: What does this have to do with me? What and how do I want to teach?

In his third year as a TA in astronomy, a graduate student observed, "Now I am teaching the way I want to. I know who I am in the context of the course. I used to feel overawed by the professor, and last year I tied myself down with detailed notes on what to cover in class. This year I know how all the pieces fit together, and I have thought out the material well in advance. Now I can be more myself. I feel free to put my own personality into teaching." Another TA discovered that she had taught her best class one day when she felt totally unprepared. Not being constrained by a set of written notes, she was teaching in her own voice. Trusting herself with the material and listening genuinely to what students were saying, she was free to manage the discussion gently, without forcing it to fit a preconceived structure.

Asking for Help

TAs who have begun to recognize their own teaching voices can respond to feedback that is reflective and challenging and that helps them examine their experiences of teaching and develop according to their own strengths and interests. Earlier, when they are just starting to encounter the complexities of the teacher-student relationship and orient themselves to the classroom, they may seek more directive and confirming advice that tells them how to perform specific teaching functions and lets them know they are performing acceptably. Even then, as lost as they may feel, many TAs do not want simply to be told what to do. Reflecting on what TAs go through, Rachel said, "They need someone there with them to help them process the experience and offer support. You don't want someone to tell you what's right. You want what you do to be yourself."

At every point, the appropriate focus for anyone who would help TAs is not only their observable teaching performances but also their personal experiences of teaching. An observer may notice that a TA who is having difficulty explaining chemistry problems needs to organize the presentation better. The TA's view, however, may be that he or she does not know enough chemistry to teach it, that students do not ask questions when they are confused, or that elementary chemistry is just too boring to explain. Again, the TA may be less concerned with clear presentation than with covering enough material or handling a difficult student. To give help effectively, the observer must address the problems the TA perceives and considers worth solving. Not until those problems have been heard will the TA be open to exploring the issues the observer raises. The TA still may not pay attention to the observer's suggestions if these issues do not seem interesting. Similarly, even if the observer has only praise, the TA may need to bring up some difficulty before hearing it. Nevertheless, it is important to acknowledge the TA's strengths and respond to the TA's individual voice; too much advice can smother enthusiasm and spontaneity.

The TA's own perspective is crucial, not just for solving problems but also for getting help in the first place. Rachel's progress with her problems concerning discussion depended on her willingness to work on them. She had her class videotaped and reviewed it with a teaching consultant, on her own initiative. Assistance is often extended to TAs through orientations, training sessions, and classroom visits, such as are available at Stanford (Fisher, 1981). Even so, TAs are frequently reluctant to ask for help when they need or want it, and their reluctance may be completely independent of any difficulty or ease they are experiencing. Unlike a paper written for a course, teaching is never meant to be a finished, public performance; rather, it is a spontaneous, private interaction with students. TAs make themselves particularly vulnerable if they invite anyone to observe them. Cynthia, who thrived on the freedom her department allowed her in teaching and who found success and satisfaction in her performance, still reported at the end of her three-year stint as a TA that she had always felt too inhibited to ask for feedback, even though she had always wanted it. In her view, TAs are typically too fearful, proud, or stubborn to seek help, even when it is readily available. As a result, teaching can be as lonely as graduate work.

To reach TAs, help must come in flexible and varied forms. Whether it is an independent center, like the one Rachel consulted, or a departmental resource, like the teaching-support committee Kevin served on during his fourth year as a TA, a potential source of help must be both inviting and tactfully persistent in its approach, as well as accessible and responsive to spontaneous requests. TAs benefit most from getting help with problems that arise in the immediate context of actual teaching. Such help can accelerate learning from experience and empower the TA to do a satisfactory and satisfying job.

References

Fairbank, J. K. "Small-Group Instruction." Videotaped panel presentation for the Professional Training Series. Cambridge, Mass.: Harvard–Danforth Center for Teaching and Learning, Harvard University, 1982.

Fisher, M. *Teaching at Stanford.* Stanford, Calif.: Center for Teaching and Learning, Stanford University, 1981.

Kasulis, T. P. "Questioning." In M. M. Gullette (Ed.), *The Art and Craft of Teaching.* Cambridge, Mass.: Harvard–Danforth Center for Teaching and Learning, Harvard University, 1982.

Katz, J., and Hartnett, R. T. *Scholars in the Making: The Development of Graduate and Professional Students.* Cambridge, Mass.: Ballinger, 1976.

Perry, W. G., Jr. *Forms of Intellectual and Ethical Development in the College Years.* New York: Holt, Rinehart & Winston, 1968.

Walters, P. "The Stresses of Being a Beginning Teacher." Videotaped panel presentation for the Professional Training Series. Cambridge, Mass.: Harvard–Danforth Center for Teaching and Learning, Harvard University, Harvard University, 1982.

Westheimer, F. "Small-Group Instruction." Videotaped panel presentation for the Professional Training Series. Cambridge, Mass.: Harvard–Danforth Center for Teaching and Learning, Harvard University, 1982.

John Boehrer is associate director of the Video Laboratory in the Harvard–Danforth Center for Teaching and Learning at Harvard University.

Ellen Sarkisian is associate director of the Video Laboratory in the Harvard–Danforth Center for Teaching and Learning at Harvard University.

Picking the right kind of program for TA development entails careful deliberation of the best location for it and of the different forces that may support or oppose it.

Programs for TAs in the Context of Campus Policies and Priorities

Richard Smock
Robert Menges

At one large public Midwestern university during the fall semester of 1982, 1,617 graduate teaching assistants taught 2,880 course sections out of 7,540 total sections, about 38 percent. There is no question that these part-time instructors, most often teaching in order to meet the expenses of their degree work, play an important part in creating the instructional atmosphere that an undergraduate experiences, particularly during the early undergraduate years. While college and university faculties of tomorrow will be recruited from the graduate assistants who are teaching today, programs to prepare them for their teaching duties are too often absent or haphazard. Therefore, issues related to increasing the teaching proficiency of graduate assistants are crucially important to the educational enterprise.

The Institution's Obligation

Until the last few years, about 50 percent of new doctoral graduates accepted academic positions in higher education. Even though this percentage may be declining (Cartter, 1976; Allen, 1982), most of the doctoral graduates in many disciplines will continue to view teaching as their primary career goal. In departments where this is not the case, time devoted to helping TAs become

J. D. W. Andrews (Ed.). *Strengthening the Teaching Assistant Faculty.* New Directions for Teaching and Learning, no. 22. San Francisco: Jossey-Bass, June 1985.

better teachers can be justified because increasing their knowledge and skills related to communicating information in small groups is an important educational and professional goal in itself.

Whether or not TAs intend to follow university careers, universities are faced with an ethical requirement to provide the highest-quality instruction for their undergraduate students. This ethical issue is not being ignored; *The Journal of Higher Education* recently devoted an entire issue to the question of ethics and the academic profession. Many of the questions raised were related to increasing pressure for a professional code of ethics that would include teaching as an academic responsibility. Writing in that issue, Schurr (1982) said any code that might be developed must provide for effective teaching and evaluation.

One means for meeting the ethical requirements and achieving quality instruction is by assisting TAs to become effective teachers. A significant advantage of concentrating faculty-development efforts on TAs is that they still have some of the role expectations of students and are reasonably receptive to instruction about teaching.

Comments from the Disciplines

Individual faculty members in many disciplines are concerned about the need for better prepared TAs. These faculty serve as gadflies to their disciplines by presenting papers at annual meetings and publishing in specialized journals. Representative of this group, Yoder and Hugenberg (1980), reporting TA training practices among 136 speech communication departments in this country, gently chided their readers: "A fairly common assumption of communication departments—and college teaching in general—is that if the teacher knows the subject matter, then he/she will be able to communicate that material to the students. Interestingly, only about one-fifth of the [TAs] are assigned to courses primarily on the basis of their content area of study. [TA] knowledge of content area seems to be a secondary criterion for course assignments" (p. 16). The authors also remark that research skills, not teaching skills, are emphasized in most of the graduate schools across the nation, even though "in virtually no other job would a person be expected to perform well without training" (p. 16). Staton-Spicer and Nyquist (1979) neatly summarize the importance of TAs to their discipline: "In speech communication, in particular, graduate TAs tend to perform a major portion of the teaching at the introductory level, since historically the discipline has been committed to small performance courses and has utilized TAs to cover the required number of sections" (p. 199).

In a survey of practices within English departments, Eble (1972) concluded that "English is ahead of some disciplines in the specific pedagogical training and supervision it gives to graduate assistants" but that "its efforts might be characterized as largely defensive in nature. The need is to ensure some uniformity of practices among inexperienced teachers and to reduce the possible cries of outrage from students and parents and administrators." A sampling of twenty-seven representative Ph.D.-granting institutions revealed that among only a dozen was teaching regarded as an important part of training for many Ph.D. candidates in English. In about a third of the departments, freshman composition was the only course taught by TAs; in the majority, supervisory programs did exist, but with small involvement of regular staff members at all ranks. Eble's study also notes that a survey of ninety-four leading universities granting Ph.D. degrees in biology revealed that 66 percent provided no special prior training to TAs.

A political science faculty member recently wrote, "While the methodology of political science remains a sacrosanct topic for us, the methodology of teaching occasions only a yawn or a bored look" (Noonan, 1982, p. 106). Noonan then encourages her fellow political scientists to look with more favor on programs to present systematic instruction in teaching. The climate for participating in programs that treat teaching as anything other than an art form varies markedly across individuals and disciplines. Another political scientist reminds us that many professors "view such training with considerable and often well-justified skepticism. . . . They believe that it is denuded of substance, [and] elevates technique above content" (Paletz, 1977, p. 136).

These varying and even contradictory points of view are representative of the larger literature concerned with efforts to improve TA teaching. This variety of attitudes illustrates the difficulty surrounding policy decisions related to TA development programs. Comprehensive universitywide programs to help TAs become more effective teachers are an ideal still to be achieved on most campuses.

Institutional Programs

For our purposes, we define *program* as a set of formally organized activities, including attention to the issues of teaching, learning, and student assessment. Our minimal definition excludes professors' ordinary weekly meetings with the TAs when such meetings are limited to specifics of a particular course. It also excludes departmental orientation meetings held by departments, even though a few words about teaching may be said during orientation.

Programs to help TAs become better teachers appear to be increasing. Where they are, what they include, and how they are assessed depends on the policies, priorities, and contexts of individual campuses. Furthermore, program features are tempered by serendipitous events and influenced by particular individuals in an organizational structure.

Location of Programs for TAs

Introducing programs to improve the teaching of TAs in research-oriented universities represents a change in current practice. Because universities are traditionally conservative institutions and professors are deeply socialized to current methods of professional preparation (Hefferlin, 1969), establishing credible programs is a challenge. Crucial to the successful development and continuation of such programs is the decision about their organizational location. Location has a direct impact on the program's credibility, flexibility to meet the variety of needs presented by disciplines, visibility on the campus, and feasibility in relation to logistical and resource issues.

We suggest several possible locations: the office of a top academic administrator; individual colleges; a college or a school of education; or simply individual departments, especially those with large-enrollment introductory undergraduate courses using many TAs. In specific courses where size makes it practical, some individual instructors may even develop their own TA programs. Each location has advantages and disadvantages, which we shall examine below. We do recognize that there are usually constraints in the choice of location. At large, research-oriented universities, it is very likely that several programs in several locations will operate concurrently. The issue of location becomes important when we wish to reach more TAs or increase the impact of TA programs in other ways. Procedural issues are also affected by organizational location. For instance, programs may be required or voluntary, for credit or not for credit, presented by professional educators or by discipline-oriented faculty.

Programs Offered by Individual Course Instructors

Meetings between faculty members and the TAs who help them are probably the most common form of TA training on campus. We consider here, as stated earlier, not meetings dealing with individual courses but only those activities of individual faculty members that treat issues of teaching, learning, and student assessment, including teaching methods. In many departments, the norms of faculty behavior discourage discussion of teaching per se. In other departments, particularly those associated with secondary teacher education programs, there may be faculty who can offer students a broad perspective on issues of teaching.

Advantages. Complete control of the program is in the hands of an instructor; therefore, content and method can be perfectly integrated according to the ideas of that instructor. Such integration enhances the credibility of the program in the eyes of TAs. Working relationships between the TAs and the professor are close, and so such logistics as scheduling meetings and obtaining materials derive from personal contacts and bypass support staff and administrative hierarchies. In this setting, the question of whether activities are required or voluntary need not even arise; participation is assured by day-to-day contact and natural expectations. This kind of program can be the least expensive in terms of dollars, although certainly not in terms of faculty time. It seems desirable to locate such programs in departments that have faculty who are knowledgeable about instructional concerns, as well as about their subject matter; that have courses requiring large numbers of TAs; and that are prepared to support programmatic efforts to improve their teaching.

Disadvantages. When the individual instructor is in charge and there is no description of the course content or of the responsibilities of the instructor to the TAs, then there is no TA program outside of that defined by the person running the course. Large introductory courses using many TAs for instruction are often the same courses through which faculty are rotated as they gain seniority. Thus, lacking leadership continuity, the TA program can fluctuate greatly in quality from year to year. Programs are not systematic over time, since faculty assume their responsibility with varying completeness.

In most departments, there are one or two large courses that use most of the TAs, with a smaller number assigned to individual faculty or to independent courses with smaller enrollments. The latter TAs are liable to receive less assistance with their teaching, since individual faculty-run programs usually do not serve all TAs in the department.

Programs Offered by Individual Departments

As a requirement for the Ph.D., some departments require all graduate students to teach one or two semesters, while others strongly encourage but do not require teaching experience. Occasionally these departments offer a for-credit course on methods of teaching the discipline. In other instances, a program for which no credit is given will be required before or during the time that the graduate student teaches.

Advantages. Waltzer (1983), a political scientist, describes the department as "the essential and operative intellectual and moral community for promoting and enforcing the canons of good teaching. . . . [Departments] continue to provide the dynamic but controlled environment suitable for. . . the liberal and professional education of students" (pp. 17, 20). A departmental program is visible evidence to TAs that teaching is important. These programs make it more likely that all TAs, not just those assigned to large-enrollment courses, will receive assistance with their teaching. Departmental programs are more likely to have continuity and to achieve institutionalization than are programs offered by individual instructors, especially when the programs are offered for credit and required of all TAs. For-credit courses also make TAs feel easier about devoting time to them.

Whether for credit or not, departmental programs are controlled by the discipline; the content and the methods are based in the discipline and reflect the discipline's beliefs about learning and teaching. Integration of content and method can be achieved efficiently in this situation, and faculty support can be gained more easily.

Departmental programs are usually taught by faculty within the discipline, which is another factor enhancing their credibility. Departmental programs may also be designed and monitored by a faculty teaching committee, thereby involving more people and incorporating a broader range of educational ideas. Where national projects exist to improve teaching within the discipline, excellent educational materials may be easily available.

Disadvantages. Many problems with departmental programs are caused by the faculty's greater interest in research than in teaching. Teaching programs may be slighted in terms of resources, time, and commitment. Program responsibility may settle on one person who takes a special interest in teaching. It is tempting for the departmental administrator to assign the program to a faculty member who is not being productive in research, but this move does not necessarily benefit the program. Departments also vary greatly in their command of resources; some are rich in overhead funds produced through grants and research contracts, while others have little such money. This disparity may be reflected in program quality. Another disadvantage of departmental programs is that faculty with teaching experience may be well represented, but faculty with knowledge of current educational research and innovative teaching practices may not exist in the department. Thus, programs may be relatively limited in scope and presented in a way that preserves the status quo in teaching styles and methods; in departments where the quality of teaching is haphazard, another generation of poorly prepared graduates may be the result. Finally, departmentally required teaching programs may be established for reasons not directly tied to instructional skills. For example, students can gain federal tax benefits on stipends awarded in programs that require teaching as a condition for obtaining the degree. Programs established for such reasons are likely to receive minimal human and material support from the department.

Programs Offered by a College of Education Serving the Whole Campus

Because the impetus for TA programs often originates among faculty in a college of education, this seems to be a natural location for a program. Education is the domain of people who spend their professional lives researching teaching and learning, so that research interest and teaching interest are likely to match most closely in this college.

Advantages. As the centers of research activities related to teaching, colleges or schools of education offer easy access to expertise, as well as the possibility of more flexibility in using that expertise through joint and part-time appointments. A program housed in a college of education is in a friendly environment. Such a program enables the college to offer important services to the campus at large and can help establish the college as a campuswide resource. Budgets may be protected when a TA program is in the college of education because programs here are apt to be seen as more important to the college than are similar programs in other colleges. Recognition that teaching itself is a proper subject to teach eliminates the defensive battles that could arise in other settings. In a college of education, educators are credible people.

Disadvantages. In research-oriented universities, colleges of education are typically among the least prestigious on campus and may have some difficulty reaching TAs in departments outside the college. Many disciplines hold stereotypes of educational experts as proponents of a rather extreme view of behaviorism, interested only in the observable skills of teaching. Thus, intellectual credibility automatically granted to practitioners of other disciplines must be earned by academics in education. This problem is emphasized when the TA program is housed in a college of education. Another disadvantage is that academic representatives of the disciplines may not associate themselves with programs in a college of education as readily as they may with programs housed elsewhere. This reluctance is not unanimous, and many fine scholars are associated with such programs, but other locations are probably more desirable for attracting scholars from other disciplines.

Programs Offered by Individual Colleges

Often, colleges other than a college of education have housed TA programs, for a number of reasons. A college housing an audiovisual unit, for instance, may make efforts to improve TA teaching because of the special interest of a college administrator or because an interested faculty member has written a proposal for funds to establish this activity.

Advantages. Support from the dean and other college administrators increases the credibility as well as the visibility of a program housed in a college. It can express the dean's interest and support of teaching. Since the program will serve more than one department, teaching specialists from a variety of disciplines may be included, and the program may be large enough to have educational specialists on the staff or serving as consultants. Location in a college allows a program to concentrate on activities compatible with the type and style of teaching most common to that college. In contrast to programs offered at the departmental level, programs with full-time staff can offer services to the college throughout the academic year. These programs are also more likely to have continuity, since they usually are staffed by specialists and are immune from the turnover associated with individual course assignments in departments.

Disadvantages. TA program budgets that are embedded in individual college budgets are not only in direct competition with departmental budgets but also fairly visible. When money becomes tight, such programs are easy targets. College programs, except those found in colleges of education, are seldom expected to serve departments outside the college; thus, the campus is likely to be unevenly served, depending on the importance attached to teaching by each dean. There may also be administrative and overhead costs beyond those of programs housed in departments, because college programs are apt to be larger and to be headed by paid administrators with clerical assistance. Special offices are likely to be needed, whereas departmental programs are often conducted from a faculty member's office. All these conditions may or may not be acceptable to departments within a college or across the campus. Another disadvantage is that college-based programs, as well as more centrally located programs, are apt to be seen as reflecting administrative rather than academic interests and may have difficulty gaining credibility.

Programs Offered Through a Central Administrative Office

For historical as well as logical reasons, the most common location for TA programs is in a unit reporting to a central university administrator. Testing and audiovisual centers (begun years ago) and instructional improvement and staff-development activities (founded over the last two decades) are often in central locations to provide service to the whole university. TA programs are but one recent addition to this list of services.

Advantages. A central unit can make a program equally available to all TAs on campus and is efficient with respect to fiscal accountability, development of instructional materials, scheduling of various program activities, and coordination of activities with other instructional support units. A central unit can efficiently develop and deliver programs to serve special populations, such as foreign TAs or TAs teaching laboratory selections. A program reporting to central university administrators is a visible demonstration of the university's interest and commitment to teaching, and it permits independent hiring practices to find the best faculty and staff for TA development. Because central administrators are often in touch with state legislators, boards of control, and parents of students, as well as being courts of last resort for student complaints, they are usually more sensitive to the importance of undergraduate teaching than faculty and administrators are at departmental levels. Thus, they are more likely to establish and support formal efforts to improve the teaching of TAs. University funding also makes it unnecessary to rely on the multiple budgeting processes that operate in departments and colleges and can ensure continuity of quality and services.

Disadvantages. Professional staff can too easily lose touch with activities of the teaching faculty and remove themselves from the day-to-day teaching issues important in particular disciplines. They may not become part of the informal network where many educational issues are resolved. Some educational specialists operating from a central location may develop programs that reflect only one educational philosophy or one psychological learning theory; the program is then credible only for those departments that subscribe wholeheartedly to that view. Even if a program starts out broadly based in terms of learning theory and philosophy, it is easy to lose that initial flexibility and become standardized, over time, if staff are in a central unit. Finally, some departments may use the central program to justify their avoidance of committing departmental resources (either money or faculty time) to the preparation of their own TAs.

Criteria for Assessing TA Programs

As university budgets become leaner, program accountability becomes increasingly important. Service activities, such as programs to improve teaching, are especially vulnerable. It is important to establish appropriate criteria for assessing the value of TA programs on campus and to plan program development accordingly. These criteria should reflect campus policies and priorities.

The overall criterion is how well the university meets its obligation to help all TAs achieve teaching proficiency. Individual programs, whether in departments or at higher administrative levels, should be judged on their contributions to meeting that obligation. We discuss here five subsidiary criteria: accessibility, perceived usefulness, documented impact, feasibility, and academic compatibility. The linkages between criteria and program location will vary among universities; certainly, though, the two are interactive.

Accessibility. Accessibility is an insufficient condition for program success, but it is one measure of the degree to which the university is meeting its ethical requirements, both to undergraduates receiving instruction and to TAs providing it. Departments with heavy enrollments of education majors (for example, foreign language departments) are likely as a matter of routine to give TAs opportunities to learn how to teach. The ethical requirement is better met, however, when all TAs in all departments have equal access to the activities and resources of programs suitable to individual disciplines and backed by sufficient administrative commitment to ensure continuity. This criterion asks, "Are programs easily available, and are they available to all TAs?"

Every department need not be served by the same program (except, perhaps, in the case of programs designed to meet the teaching needs of specific TA groups, such as foreign teaching assistants). In fact, it is probably unrealistic to expect universality from any program, since a wide variety of attitudes, philosophies of teaching, priorities, and teaching goals exists on most campuses.

Perceived Usefulness. Programs that are accessible but not perceived as useful can hardly be considered successful. Programs may be useful for a variety of reasons to a variety of groups, and all groups can express reasons for their satisfaction or lack of satisfaction. TAs may find the programs useful to them as teachers, and faculty and department administrators may reflect the satisfaction of the TAs in their own judgments of programs. Other administrators may consider a TA program valuable because it demonstrates a commitment that is visible to constituencies outside the university or that reflects their own concern.

Since opinions differ so much about which activities are most beneficial to TAs, usefulness can be judged in at least three ways. One is to obtain perceptions of the credibility of program content, format, and staff. A second way is to examine the uses departments make of a given program: Are teaching assignments adjusted or additional teaching practice initiated, depending on the results? Still a third measure of perceived usefulness is the proportion of TAs who participate in the program—a powerful measure, but only when attendance is voluntary.

The decision to require TA participation is an important one. On the one hand, voluntary attendance must be useful to TAs, and steady or increasing involvement becomes an excellent indicator of usefulness. On the other hand, there are powerful reasons for requiring participation. First of all, required programs ensure good attendance. Increased tuition and other educational costs, as well as ethical considerations for undergraduates, require us to do all we can to promote high instructional standards. Given the demands of graduate education, it is unrealistic to expect voluntary time commitments except from the most dedicated. If participation is helpful to some TAs, fairness demands that all TAs share equally in the benefits. These are issues that departments face when making choices between voluntary and required programs. Similar reasoning can be applied to the equally important question of whether a college or a university should require all departments to develop or participate in a TA program. However these issues are resolved, perceptions of usefulness can play an important part in determining continued support for the program.

Documented Impact. While the criterion of usefulness relates to perceptions of value, *impact* refers more specifically to effects on teaching: "Is there reason to believe that teaching is improved as a result of this program?" TA reports of satisfaction with a program's usefulness are valuable but insufficient. Such reports may indicate that the program helped relieve anxiety, but not necessarily that it increased teaching proficiency. Securing solid evidence that TAs actually teach better or that their students actually learn more is one of the most difficult tasks facing current educational researchers. Carroll (1980), in an excellent review of recent research on TA programs, expressed surprise at the "limited extent of empirical research on the effects of such training" (p. 167) and called for increased efforts to assess the results of TA development programs. Less rigorous data may be acceptable, or in some cases it may be necessary to accept them, but the question itself cannot and should not be dodged. Only a questionable program fails to identify, at least minimally, anecdotal information from students, TAs, or faculty in the informal communication network of faculty and administrators. And, of course, the more adequately such evidence is documented, the better the impact criterion is met.

Feasibility. TA development programs should be examined for feasibility in terms of dollar costs, time required, and logistics. Each of these issues is affected by program location. Dollar costs of a centrally located and funded program are subject to attack if they are perceived to be out of line with expenditures for services. When the costs of the program are combined with those of other central units, however, they are not so apt to be noticed. Costs of departmental programs are smaller to begin with and usually are controlled and spent by faculty; thus, they are less controversial. If a university relies wholly on departmentally based programs, however, rich departments will fare better than poor ones. In general, dollar costs of a TA program are one reflection of a university's priorities.

All TA programs require a time commitment from faculty or professional specialists, as well as from the TAs themselves. Programs that make unreasonable time demands fail the test of feasibility.

Programs ranked high in terms of the other criteria discussed here can still fail if they are too complex logistically. For instance, TA classroom videotapes are used in a number of programs. Scheduling times with TAs and moving videotape equipment and operators to the right rooms at the right times is a complex operation that demands careful attention to detail. Too many breakdowns in the system make it so unfeasible that alternative arrangements (such as special videotaping classrooms placed around the campus) need to be considered.

Academic Compatibility. This criterion asks, "Are the program activities and content compatible with the academic image of the institution?" The typical institution strives to project a coherent image to its constituencies, and that image should be reflected in its programs for TAs. In research-oriented universities, for example, the integrity of the Ph.D. as a research degree has a high priority. Practical or applied courses, which are seen as diluting the theoretical and methodological quality of that degree, will be resisted; programs perceived as threatening faculty autonomy or departmental independence will also be opposed.

Other types of institutions attempt to project different images, and their programs for TAs must reflect compatible notions of academic respectability. In general, the programs most likely to be successful are based on a strong intellectual rationale and rely on empirical evidence for developing activities. If programs do not satisfy the criterion of academic compatibility, then their accessibility, perceived usefulness, and feasibility will be insufficient to win the support of administrators and of the most influential faculty on campus. Furthermore, no evidence of impact will persuade faculty and administrators who find the program incompatible with the institution's academic image. Such programs ultimately have low credibility and remain vulnerable to negative financial pressures.

Searching for the Optimal Mix

Programs that meet these five subsidiary criteria have been developed within each of the organizational locations we have discussed: individual faculty, departments, colleges, and central administrative units. Most large campuses probably have programs at more than one of these locations. To maximize the advantages and compensate for the disadvantages of each location, some mix of programs is desirable.

At the University of Illinois at Urbana–Champaign, the mix includes programs offered by individual faculty, by departments, and by a centrally located unit in cooperation with departments. At this university, as at others, there is no exact count of the number of programs offered by individual faculty or by departments acting independently, but together they certainly would far outnumber the programs developed through joint planning between departments and the central unit. The central unit has made cooperative planning with departments a key feature of its TA programs; during the 1983–1984 academic year, for example, cooperative programs were offered in twenty-two departments. The degree of interaction between central unit staff and departmental faculty varied according to department commitment and preference. Some TA programs are taught both by departmental faculty and by central staff. In other departments, programs are arranged through an administrative secretary, with no direct faculty involvement at all.

A discipline-based program is attractive partly because a department has an interpersonal dimension that can enhance effectiveness. If a program is jointly developed, staff representing the central unit must develop their credibility. It is easier to do that on a departmental basis than within a total college or over a whole campus. Personal friendships, compatible views of education, and matches in scholarly style influence the ability to develop and offer effective programs. Those factors do change across departments, but they can be accommodated by knowledgeable and flexible program staff.

Central units are staffed with people who claim special educational expertise. These people must realize that the need for pedagogical assistance from educational experts is perceived and accepted to varying degrees by departments. If programs are developed cooperatively with departments, central staff can become intimately acquainted with how particular problems of teaching are discussed and with the psychological and philosophical beliefs about teaching held by department members.

The strongest programs are apt to develop when central unit staff can communicate appropriate educational principles in the language and style of each academic area. Such programs avoid inappropriate, reductionist, skill-based approaches. Bruner (1982) reminds us that those who believe teaching is simply a matter of skill mastery are people who trivialize and oversimplify teaching. He says that education should "partake of the spirit of a forum, of negotiation, of the recreating of meaning" (p. 840). Programs developed cooperatively in that spirit are programs that will find the strongest support and acceptance.

References

Allen, R. J., "Non-Facts, Assumptions, and Approaches in American Graduate Education." In F. Jacobs and R. Allen (Eds.), *Expanding the Missions of Graduate and Professional Education,* New Directions for Experiential Learning, no. 15. San Francisco: Jossey-Bass, 1982.

Bruner, J. "The Language of Education." *Social Research,* 1982, *49* (4), 835–853.

Carroll, J. G. "Effects of Training Programs for University Teaching Assistants." *The Journal of Higher Education,* 1980, *51* (2), 167–183.

Cartter, A. M. *Ph.D.'s and the Academic Labor Market.* New York: McGraw-Hill, 1976.

Eble, K. E. "Preparing College Teachers of English." *College English,* 1972, *33* (4), 385–406.

Hefferlin, J. L. *Dynamics of Academic Reform.* San Francisco: Jossey-Bass, 1969.

Noonan, N. C. "Review: The Political Scientist and the Craft of Teaching." *Teaching Political Science,* 1982, *9* (2), 106–108.

Paletz, D. L. "Teacher Education in Political Science Graduate Programs." *Teaching Political Science,* 1977, *4* (2), 131–144.

Schurr, G. M. "Toward a Code of Ethics for Academics." *The Journal of Higher Education,* 1982, *53* (3), 318–334.

Staton-Spicer, A. Q., and Nyquist, J. L. "Improving the Teaching Effectiveness of Graduate Teaching Assistants." *Communication Education,* 1979, *28* (3), 199–205.

Waltzer, H. "Providing for the Development, Preservation, and Transmission of Knowledge—The Department." *Change Magazine,* 1983, *15* (5), 16–20.

Yoder, D. D., and Hugenberg, L. W. "A Survey of Inservice Teacher Training Programs for Graduate Teaching Assistants in Basic Communication Courses." Paper presented at the annual meeting of the Speech Communication Association, New York City, November 12-15, 1980. (ERIC No. ED207-106)

Richard Smock is head of the Course Development Division of the Office of Instructional Development at the University of Illinois, Urbana.

Robert Menges is professor of education and program director of the Center for the Teaching Professions, Northwestern University.

Teaching by graduate assistants is often affected by a confusing
interplay of autonomy and authority in the TA-professor relationship.

Improving the Working Relationship Between Professor and TA

Tom Wilson
Jeanie Stearns

Analysis of the TA-Professor Relationship

The promise of the TA-professor relationship is that, without any added formal requirements, the TA one way or another will learn from supervising professors whatever he or she needs to know about teaching. Such training can proceed personally, informally, and individually. As we see it, however, that promise is all too often an empty one. The relationship between TAs and the professors who direct the courses they work in is a confused and confusing mixture of tacit autonomy and reserved authority.

The tacit autonomy extended to TAs in this relationship is rooted in an implicit belief: that demonstrated knowledge of subject matter confers the ability to teach it. There is a corresponding norm: Except when required for formal promotion and tenure reviews, criticism and advice about a colleague's teaching is definitely bad form. For the most part, the same norm is applied to TAs: Unless their teaching becomes a problem, it usually is not going to be a subject of much direct interchange between professor and TA.

J. D. W. Andrews (Ed.). *Strengthening the Teaching Assistant Faculty.* New Directions
for Teaching and Learning, no. 22. San Francisco: Jossey-Bass, June 1985.

Most departments, course directors, and TAs are too busy to attempt replacing business-as-usual staff meetings with more direct attention to pedagogy. Then, too, it is often less time-consuming and troublesome simply to withhold a teaching appointment than to spot an individual TA's problems early and provide assistance in overcoming them. And, to give course directors their due, they themselves are seldom experts in *teaching* (however expert as *teachers* some of them may be), nor are TAs always grateful for directors' attention to instructional skills.

This apparently collegial situation of tacit autonomy is complicated by what we have called reserved authority, because in truth TAs are not totally free to pursue their own courses; indeed, their courses are not their own. TAs are almost always relative novices, and in the academic hierarchy, the TA is subject to the authority of the lecturer or course director in whose name he or she teaches and on whose recommendation he or she depends for continued teaching assignments. Nevertheless—however decorously such authority may be reserved and however rarely resorted to—it is there to be exercised, as judged necessary.

To add to the confusion, little of what faculty expect of TAs in the classroom is expressed explicitly, directly, or formally. The task may be clear enough: to be there, conduct labs, lead discussion sections, write and/or grade exams or quizzes, assign and/or read papers, hold office hours as stated, and so on. How, and especially how else, to perform these tasks is likely never to be addressed. Some departments, it is true, conduct beginning-of-the-year orientations, at which teaching is discussed, but only rarely does a department extend any attention to teaching, beyond this sort of hortatory introduction.

Something else also contributes to the confusing interplay of autonomy and authority in the TA-professor relationship: However benign, downplayed, or egalitarian this relationship may seem, the two people in it are also involved in another, more encompassing and consequential relationship—that of professor and graduate student. The TA may not be the directing faculty member's student, but he or she is a student in that faculty member's department and thus his or her future career prospects are at least tangentially affected by that faculty member's asssessment.

From the interplay of tacit autonomy and reserved authority emerges a subtle control, communicated by signals rather than by direct messages. There is often little or no sense that faculty have more than a passing responsibility for their graduate students' teaching; it is considered enough to direct their scholarly work, to teach them the subject rather than how to teach it. Yet the threat of consequences, if teaching performance is insufficient, always hangs implicitly over the TA. This amounts to a double bind: Teach as best you can with minimal supervision, since teaching is not that important, but teach in a way that satisfies the director of your course, because the consequences of displeasing your director may affect your pursuit of a career. In short, don't try to succeed, but be careful not to fail. As a result, TAs often pass through a formative period of learning to dissociate themselves from much of what they are doing. They learn to identify with their scholarly work and treat teaching as a necessary evil. Future professors among them, of course, are likely to be marked by this experience.

Lest this analysis seems to present a totally negative picture of what goes on between TAs and professors we want to stress that many enduring and rewarding relationships also develop; the main virtue of university training is rooted in them. Such bonding, however, occurs more by chance or by individual faculty disposition than by deliberate university policy or behavior. And, in a profession where scholarship is privileged over teaching, scholarship is far more likely than teaching to provide the incentive for bonding.

We believe that more explicit discussion of TAs' actual functions and of their relationships with directing faculty would help make positive bonding less a matter of accident and more a result of careful, purposive concern. Unless faculty know what they are doing with TAs, it seems unlikely that effective teaching or learning about teaching will occur.

An Argument for Change

We believe that significant changes can be made in the TA-professor relationship by opening its underlying premises to explicit discussion. In fact, this may be the only way in which lasting change can occur.

Often, the relationship between tacit autonomy and reserved authority amounts to what Argyris (1976, 1982) calls a "theory-in-use": an implicit model that can be inferred from behavior but may differ sharply from the actor's "espoused theory." An observer can employ the inferred theory-in-use to predict the actor's behavior, but if the actor's espoused theory says something else, those with whom the actor deals may be misled. Moreover, any attempt to discuss the situation may simply elicit the espoused theory, thus further confusing all concerned. If an individual also has defensive motives for resisting such discussion, there will be still more barriers to open discussion.

On the basis of extensive management studies, Argyris has also suggested that a certain attitude toward working relationships is especially likely to create such barriers. This attitude involves several key assumptions about how working relationships should be conducted. These are that the parties involved must (1) achieve a purpose, as defined unilaterally by the person in charge, (2) "win," (3) suppress negative feelings, and (4) emphasize rationality. This cluster of assumptions has been labeled Model I by Argyris. It is an extremely common model for relationships in most sorts of organizations, and the TA-professor working relationship is no exception.

Each variable with Model I has important consequences for the person, other individuals, and the environment. The behavior produced is designed to control the environment and situations unilaterally, control the task, protect the self, and protect others from being hurt. These strategies in turn produce defensive and closed behaviors, reduce valid feedback, and reduce free choice. Under such conditions, people rarely seek genuine information about their own behavior. They tend to be diplomatic, play it safe, not upset others, and covertly collude to prevent the raising of issues that may challenge the way business is conducted. Because fresh information is rarely introduced, there is no basis for creating a new approach even when one is needed.

The alternative to such constriction is an open communication system, in which the participants continually re-examine the governing variables of their system. Argyris calls this a Model II environment. In such an environment, one seeks to discuss the undiscussable, make explicit the implicit, and question premises. We believe that the problem of control and authority in TA-professor relationships can be dealt with only when it becomes the subject of Model II-type dialogue, rather than remaining out of bounds, as in Model I.

The notion of questioning basic premises is hardly new to higher education: The examined life has been considered the essence of true learning ever since Socrates. In practice, though, such scrutiny has not extended to the interpersonal interactions of academics themselves, especially with respect to teaching. Argyris's term for the examined life is "double-loop learning": One learns not only about the situations illuminated by one's premises but also about what lies beyond them. Such learning can be gained only by stepping outside the premises themselves.

For example, if a novice TA has absorbed beliefs that a teacher is (1) always in charge of his or her own classroom (tacit autonomy), (2) must be rational at all times, and (3) needs to suppress negative emotions, then the TA will have no way of communicating a feeling of despair at being "abandoned" in the classroom; the professor will be cut off from true information about the TA's situation. While such information may break through from time to time, it is only when participants step outside the basic belief system that accurate and useful communication can take place. Participative information-gathering techniques (Argyris, 1976, 1982) have been developed to help organizations establish effective communication and management relationships. These methods can be applied to the relationships and communication between professors and TAs.

Just as in Model I, there are behaviors produced by Model II: sharing power with anyone who has expertise, sharing the defining of tasks and control of conditions, resisting the temptation to save face or protect self and others, seeking valid information and relevant feelings, promoting decisions open to scrutiny, and minimizing attributions and evaluations. When attributions are made, directly observable data are offered to support them; and, like other aspects of the mode, they stand subject to disconfirmation.

An Exemplary Attempt at Change

This section summarizes an attempt to evaluate and restructure the TA-professor relationship by introducing some key elements of the Model II environment described above. The project took place at the end of the spring quarter of 1980 in the humanities core course of the University of California at Irvine. This course is a year-long interdisciplinary program for freshmen. Using the lecture and discussion-group format, it is designed to introduce students to the concerns of humanists through the study of significant texts drawn from literature, philosophy, and history. Another important course function has been the teaching of English composition; close reading and analysis of textual material is complemented by essay writing.

The course is administered by a faculty member, who may or may not participate as a lecturer and who usually holds the position for two to four years. The sections are taught by TAs who are advanced graduate students and usually working on their dissertations. They are drawn from all the departments in the School of Humanities. Some faculty members also conduct section meetings.

At the time of our intervention, the course seemed to be functioning fairly well from the viewpoints of students and professor-lecturers, but TAs' dissatisfaction with workloads, conditions, and status had been expressed in previous years and had generated much faculty concern. The conception and instruction of the course in general had also been questioned by the faculty. For these reasons, the director decided to evaluate the structure and process of the course with the aid of the campus Instructional Development Service.

Evaluation and restructuring followed several explicitly announced criteria. The chief guideline was that all parties affected by the program (all those who had a stake in the proceedings) be involved in the evaluation. Involvement included participating in the processes of generating questions, collecting and reporting data, analyzing data, and planning actions. In the same spirit, it was arranged that an outside evaluator (Wilson) would team-teach a section of the course with the director, directly experiencing the working conditions (if not the working status) of the TAs. At the time of the project, Stearns was a regular TA in the course.

Faculty and TAs submitted questions they believed should be included in a questionnaire concerning the effectiveness of the program. From these questions, the evaluator constructed the questionnaire, adding a few questions based on his own direct experience. The questionnaire then was administered to all faculty, all TAs, and randomly selected sections of students from the program. Data were tabulated and summarized by the evaluator. Then, an all-day, off-campus workshop was designed by the evaluator to meet two objectives: to present the data and examine the responses, pinpointing areas of conflict and agreement among the groups; and to negotiate and plan for structural changes in identified conflict areas.

The workshop meeting—which included the course director, most of the TAs, and three professors—was highly interactive. Participants met in small groups of mixed TA and faculty membership to discuss the questionnaire results and then reported their reactions to the entire group. Since students were not included in the workshop, their opinions were inferred from their responses to the questionnaire. Initially, there was some resistance to the information, and some heated exchanges also occurred between the course director and several outspoken TAs. Some TAs also expressed resentment that so many faculty lecturers seemed to care too little to attend the workshop, but gradually the evaluator helped the group turn toward absorbing the main message of the data and synthesizing the various reactions that had been expressed. The participants then returned to their small groups and began to work on action plans, including discussion of curriculum issues and the redesign of their own staff meetings.

The areas in which faculty, TA, and student responses differed became opportunities for dialogue, leading to better relationships among participants and generating new working arrangements. The major differences are described below.

1. To a significant degree, faculty believed that discussion sessions complemented lectures, lectures were clear, and assignments enhanced learning. In responding to the questionnaire, faculty did not perceive that the program increased students' critical thinking ability as much as the students believed it did. TAs, who worked most closely with the students, were even more pessimistic about the degree of critical thinking being fostered. Discussion of these points provided a means of specifying role differences and their consequences.

2. While none of the three groups thought that there was a serious work overload in relation to the number of credit units awarded, many students did feel this issue as a problem. Students agreed most strongly with the statement that there was too much reading material to cover, with faculty disagreeing most strongly and TAs falling in between. This indication of student difficulty led to a discussion of relative tasks and workloads and contributed to a revision of course emphasis in the fall quarter.

3. Faculty and student ratings were in agreement that student reading skills had improved, yet TAs disagreed with students on this outcome. The same pattern was found with respect to broadening of student intellectual perspective. Discussion of the TAs' reasons for disagreeing helped again to emphasize TAs' heavy involvement with students and responsibility for evaluating them.

The workshop discussions arising from these three points identified a number of shared teaching concerns. Generally, the emphasis was on similar, course-related issues, but a number of personal and group resentments also emerged. The workshop format made it possible to express and deal with concerns and complaints about the organization and administration of the course, as well as with tensions among individuals.

In addition, the TAs appeared satisfied, to some extent, by the administrator's willingness to allow for their participation. The administrator noted that the desire for substantial curricular change was apparently less at issue than was participation in the administrative process itself. This result of the workshop was particularly significant, since during the year the director's efforts to open informal channels of communication with the staff had not led to similar results.

As a result of the evaluation discussion, the following changes occurred:

1. TA representatives were appointed to meet with the faculty team for the fall quarter to re-evaluate the curriculum and discuss the writing assignments.

2. Representatives were appointed to meet with the winter quarter lecturers to carry out the same function.

3. It was announced at the first staff meeting of the year that the TAs would be asked to elect a committee to act as a liaison with the administrator of the course.

4. The liaison committee and the director agreed to change the thrust of weekly staff meetings. The size of the meetings (from twenty-two to thirty individuals), and the entrenched norms of nonparticipation and superficial acquiescence that had built up over the years, had generated vastly negative reactions. Instead, the entire staff began by meeting for about ten to fifteen minutes. Then, for the next forty minutes, there were meetings of three groups, made up of TAs from the disciplines represented. The faculty and the director rotated among the groups. Observation and participants' comments suggested that this new format was very beneficial. It provided for more genuine decision making and more discussion of teaching and streamlined the administrative discussions.

5. An additional program change grew from analysis of the discrepancies among faculty, TAs, and students concerning students' progress in critical thinking. It was logically sound to give substantial weight to the views of the TAs because of their sustained direct contact with the students—especially since faculty lecturers who also taught sections tended to agree with the TAs on this point. There was general agreement that students needed work on reading, analysis, and interpretation of written material. As a result, the course was redesigned to focus on reading in the fall quarter.

What is significant about this project is that both the identification of the problem and the strategies of solution were products of a participatory, Model II-type process. Because the process elicited questions from all categories of participants and attended to differences among responses, the undiscussable found its way onto the agenda of discussion. Airing of these differences focused attention on the previously taken-for-granted fact that TAs carried the burden of work with students while having little if any input into curriculum planning and procedures.

At the same time, the participative approach described here could have been carried even farther. While the general problems raised in the discussion were approached in the spirit of Model II, this effort was incomplete, in that TAs were not included in the planning of the workshop and students were excluded from it entirely. In future efforts, correcting these two limitations would greatly enhance the participatory aspect of the process.

Nevertheless, we believe that several benefits resulted from this project. First, of course, the program was improved. Second, working conditions for everyone were enhanced by open discussion and reduction of tensions. There were also benefits directly relevant to TAs: They gained confidence by having their opinions taken seriously, learned from the experience of having to think about the design and aims of the course as a whole, and were able to participate in redesigning relationships with the course director and the professors so as to provide a more effective apprenticeship.

In carrying out many teaching consultations, we have found that the approach described above can be adapted widely; and we strongly encourage concerned course directors to institute the process of participatory restructuring.

Faculty and TA Responses to Questions About Change

On our own campus, we decided to explore receptiveness to this approach via a questionnaire survey of faculty (course directors) and TAs. We wondered how many of our respondents would see value in participative restructuring, how many would think that some less fundamental change was sufficient, and how many would be content with the current pattern. If a large number supported the status quo, we thought, we might have to conclude that attempting to get many academics to move toward Model II would be quixotic. But if a significant majority did not give these reactions — if they felt that structural change of the TA-professor relationship was desirable — then the admittedly difficult task of trying to establish Model II-type environments would at least have some sanction of informed opinion.

We distributed sixty questionnaires to TAs and twenty-one to course directors (separate but related questionnaires for the two groups), dividing the numbers equally among social sciences, math and natural sciences, and the humanities. Twenty-seven TAs and fifteen course directors completed and returned them (45 percent and 71 percent, respectively, of the total sample). The questionnaires for TAs had twenty questions; those for course directors, twenty-seven. These questions fell into the four major groupings indicated in the left-hand column of Table 1. The percentages of each group's responses

Table 1. Change Questionnaire[a]

		Yes	No
Course direction, TA situation OK as is	Profs	13 (87%)	0
	TAs	6 (22%)	14 (52%)
There should be (greater) professorial leadership, attention to TAs' teaching	Profs	9 (60%)	4 (26%)
	TAs	19 (70%)	6 (22%)
There should be a (greater) TA voice, participation in decision making	Profs	11 (73%)	2 (13%)
	TAs	17 (63%)	7 (26%)
Change to greater TA voice and participation is possible	Profs	6 (42%)	2 (13%)
	TAs	13 (48%)	11 (41%)

[a] Percentages do not always total 100 percent because equivocal or qualified responses were not included in the tabulation.

that agreed substantially with each major proposition are indicated in the body of the table.

The greatest discrepancy between TAs' and course directors' attitudes, as measured by our questionnaires, was in the first proposition, that course direction was already satisfactory. Of the course directors, 87 percent said yes, while only 22 percent of the TAs agreed. This difference is not surprising; for decision makers to be more satisfied than those subject to their decisions is certainly not unusual. A closer look at the six TA questionnaires that reflected satisfaction with course directors and the teaching situation in general reveals a significant common feature: Five of these TAs had worked in courses directed in a participatory fashion, with frank relationships and responsiveness to TAs' ideas about prevailing practices. The fourteen TAs who reported themselves clearly dissatisfied also indicated that their course directors were more authoritarian than participative, more impersonal than personal, and/or more closed than open to TA concerns. When these correspondences are taken into account, the discrepancy between course directors and TAs appears even more significant.

We also expected this difference to emerge in the responses to the next three propositions, with more course directors wishing for stronger leadership and more TAs wishing for more participatory decision making. Interestingly enough, this was not the case. Course directors and TAs split over the question of how satisfactory the current situation was, but they joined again in their attitudes about professorial leadership and TA participation in decision making. A clear majority of both groups preferred close professorial attention to TAs' teaching, structuring of TAs' work, and general exercise of authority, as well as strong TA participation in course operations.

This paradoxical result interested us greatly. Would the strong exercise of professorial leadership and authority contradict our efforts to create a participatory environment, as described in our previous discussion? Plainly, our respondents did not think so. Perhaps, though, they wanted the impossible! We began to look at this finding in terms of our earlier analysis of the current theory-in-use guiding the TA-professor relationship: that it tends to be a confusing and frustrating mixture of tacit autonomy (no firm supervision) and reserved authority (no true participatory input). What professors and TAs alike wanted, as reflected in their questionnaires, was the exact opposite of this pattern. Thus, they seemed to question the premises of the current working relationship (as Model II prescribes) and find it wanting.

On the whole, these results suggest that course directors and TAs alike want changes in the TA-professor relationship and that these changes are not disastrously incompatible. Although the faculty in our sample were clearly more satisfied with the status quo than the TAs were, the general direction of desired change was similar for both groups. There was no sign that the TAs were generally resistant to being supervised; rather, we think that re-examining the premises of the TA-professor relationship in a participatory way would lead very often to situations in which the issue of supervision versus autonomy would be mutually negotiated, thus according with the Model II concept.

We would like to add some final thoughts on change tactics. Given the value that our respondents placed on professorial leadership, it seems that if the TA-professor relationship is to change, the initiative for that change may have to be unilateral, coming from course directors and/or departments.

As those who have concerned themselves with TA training will recognize, ways to address course directors are as various as course directors are themselves and range from prosyletizing to informing to rendering logistical assistance. Some course directors or departments, resigned to benign neglect of their TAs' teaching, may respond to the salubrious shock of seeing student evaluations of TAs and TAs' evaluations of their own situations. Information describing successful TA programs in particular disciplines can also be helpful in dealing with these directors. Others, who believe that teaching styles and skills are as unchangeable as eye color and that tampering with teaching style violates nature and academic freedom, may respond to evidence of improved teaching at their own level. Some others may be directly helped with such tasks as providing videofeedback for TAs or organizing teaching workshops.

Most significantly, though, directors who become informed and persuaded of the virtues of Model II-type communication can be aided in establishing such communication with their own TAs. This solution — by involving

TAs in articulation, diagnosis, and action on their situations — would clarify the TA-professor relationship from within. It would also allow both parties to escape the Model I-type limbo of tacit autonomy and reserved authority and move toward developing more collaborative working relationships.

References

Argyris, C. *Increasing Leadership Effectiveness.* New York: John Wiley and Sons, 1976.
Argyris, C. *Reasoning, Learning, and Action.* San Francisco: Jossey-Bass, 1982.

Tom Wilson is director of the Instructional Development Service at the University of California, Irvine.

Jeanie Stearns is a program associate with the Instructional Development Service, University of California, Irvine.

The TA is not just a miniature professor. Careful consideration of the TA's unique situation with respect to students leads to recognizing the necessity for TAs to use a variety of teaching methods and course formats.

Why TA Training Needs Instructional Innovation

John D. W. Andrews

Performing the basic tasks of a TA requires a repertoire of teaching methods and class formats, many of which are unfamiliar to most TAs. Such a repertoire is needed to resolve certain recurring and baffling problems that TAs find hard to deal with in the context of lecture or recitation formats. The saying has it that if your only tool is a hammer, you are apt to go around treating everything as if it were a nail, a saying that basically describes the situation faced by a TA who has only traditional instructional methods to draw on. Accordingly, the aims of this chapter are, first, to spell out the central TA functions and how they fit into university education as a whole and, second, to present an array of innovative approaches — all of them field-tested by TAs in typical undergraduate courses — that can be employed to carry out these functions.

Core TA Functions

First, the TA is a source of personal contact and interaction with students. TAs usually teach small classes to students of about their same age, thus providing an opportunity for informal interaction with students inside and outside class. Students, especially in the earlier years, need encouragement, models, and understanding of their problems. Providing for these needs does not necessarily involve personal confidences — although it sometimes does —

J. D. W. Andrews (Ed.). *Strengthening the Teaching Assistant Faculty.* New Directions for Teaching and Learning, no. 22. San Francisco: Jossey-Bass, June 1985.

rather, it involves a demonstrated interest in students' learning motivation and progress. The element of personal contact affects student-to-student interactions, too. The TA needs to be a facilitator of group communication so that students will feel free to participate in class and make the most of their opportunities to learn from each other.

Second, the TA is in the best position to help develop higher-level thinking skills through coaching, guidance, and feedback. These skills—involving analysis, creativity, and evaluative judgment (Bloom, 1956)—cannot be fostered in large lectures, but only in Socratic interaction. The teacher must be able to observe the student thinking aloud and then help to shape this process (Whimbey and Lochhead, 1980). Students need to be as active as the teacher—for example, in writing or scientific (mathematical) problem-solving assignments; and, if we are to take seriously the rhetoric in most college catalogues, then the TA should be a vital agent in the development of critical minds. This role is doubly important, because it most strongly affects students in the lower-division years, during which crucial intellectual skills are being formed.

Finally, the TA often must provide a communication channel that helps to integrate the course. The preparation that students bring to a course is often below what a professor expects, and the degree to which a professor elaborates different topics may be beyond a student's ability to understand. Course goals may be presented vaguely or may be misunderstood because of incorrect assumptions on the part of students and professors alike. The basis of grading may be misleadingly explained or misinterpreted by students. The TA who handles section meetings for a lecture course is in the best position to see students' problems close at hand, to field most of their questions, to correct misimpressions, and often to play the major part in evaluating tests or papers and assigning grades. Thus, the TA can serve as a two-way communication channel between students and professor, making suggestions about course planning, elaborating on incompletely covered material, explaining evaluation criteria to students, and providing practice in developing critical thinking skills.

To illustrate some of the things students are looking for in their teachers, there follow some comments from a group of freshmen who took part in a TA training retreat.

> This guy knows me, you know, he understands my situation and he wants me to learn and so I want to learn. That's what the TAs gave to me last year. He cares about me. I wanted to learn more about chemistry because the TAs wanted to teach me more about chemistry. Words like "you can do it," maybe, or "this is important," or, like, "it's not as bad as it looks," that's a good one; "it looks bad now, but after a while. . ." the whole course is a psyche-out; if you can get the people to think they can learn it, they'll learn it.

I think it's establishing an environment where there's constant participation all the time. When there's a lot of lecture, you just don't get used
to raising your hand. I remember one time I raised my hand and answered a question, and I felt so ridiculous, because the whole class
turned around and stared at me.

They would put problems up on the board, and of course no one would
know how to do them, which was probably natural, but what they
showed me in particular was how to look at the problem, how to analyze it, and how to use all given data that you have, and how to make
use of that data in solving for various parts of the equation—to see how
he sets it up, how he takes the data he's given and arranges it so he can
use a simple formula to solve it. And it was by doing that over and over
again and by constantly seeing the TAs, so that they would show me if I
was going off on the wrong track, that I was eventually able to get some
kind of a method in looking at these problems.

The three TA functions—interactive learning, coaching in the higher thinking
skills, and providing a communication channel to integrate the course—stand
out quite vividly in these students' comments.

How, then, do we help TAs to carry out these functions more effectively? In our workshops, we use two major means. First, we provide a simple
but complete planning system, which the TA can use in either of two ways: to
organize his or her own section work, and to assess or analyze a course for
which he or she is serving as a TA. A second major resource for TAs is a "tool-
box" of classroom activities designed to stimulate students to take active, participative roles in the classroom.

A Course Planning Guide for TAs

The planning guide is a grid incorporating five stages. These are based
on the concept of performance objectives in learning. The guide is not a micro-
scopic analysis of behavioral outcomes, such as that advocated by Mager
(1975). Rather, it emphasizes that a course must be integrated, and it helps
TAs articulate goals in terms of tasks that students will be able to do at the end
of the course but cannot do now. Table 1 shows our planning guide.

The instructor fills in each box with the appropriate information and
thus creates a schematic course outline. We stress that planning begins with
Box 1, on the right: "How do you want students to be changed. . . ?" The guide
works across to Box 5 on the left: "How are your expectations communicated
to students?" (We sometimes call this guide the Chinese Planner, because the
planning steps, like Chinese writing, are written in right-to-left order.) When
the guide is completed, the teaching sequence can be implemented from left to

Table 1. Teaching Objectives Planning Guide

Instructions: It is in the nature of objectives, or outcomes, to arrive last, yet our concept of the outcome can have an important influence on what leads to the objective. In this sense, defining objectives is the first step in planning a learning activity. For this reason, we ask you to work in right-to-left order, beginning with question 1, in thinking through your teaching plans. The result should be a sequential model of what you intend to do, which can then be implemented from left to right, beginning with box A in the second row.

5. How are your expectations communicated to students? What is their picture of the objectives they will need to meet?	4. What about the "how" of teaching? What sorts of formats or activities will you use to help students practice the abilities needed to meet (1) and (2)?	3. What subject-matter content will you cover in order to help students meet the expectations in (1) and (2)?	2. How are these changes to be measured? What sorts of performances by students will be the criteria?	1. How do you want students to be changed as a result of this class? What will they perceive, or be able to do, that they cannot do now?
(A)	(B)	(C)	(D)	(E)

right, beginning with the introduction (A) and ending with objectives accomplished (E).

As mentioned, this model can be used by TAs to plan their own teaching work or to gain perspectives on the course as a whole and how their efforts should fit into it. One interesting way to do the latter is to interview the course professor, using the questions of Box 1; another is to preview the tests or assignments due later in the course as a way of seeing concretely how objectives are to be embodied in the measurement system (Box 2). In workshops, we often use the teaching situations of one or two TAs as examples. We begin by asking about student learning outcomes. Often, the TA is unaware of these; they have been unstated, taken for granted, put purely in terms of content, or phrased so generally that they are meaningless. Trying to deal with these questions often stimulates the TA's curiosity about the professor's answers and the possible gaps that may show up later in the course. New TAs are busy figuring out how to handle today's class, and so the end of the course (three months away) may seem remote and irrelevant. This walk-through exercise provides a needed corrective, showing that one can teach fruitfully in the present only in the light of one's destination.

Course objectives (Box 1) should deal with subject matter as well as thinking skills, and should be embodied explicitly in the measurement system (Box 2), and should be congruent with what goes on in lecture and in section. To say that the material covered (Box 3) should match the objectives seems so obvious that it scarcely needs mentioning, but it is not uncommon for students to prepare largely from lectures and then face a test based on the textbook. Thus, we stress that TAs, in helping to integrate the course, should look closely at the match between course content and measurement emphasis.

Even more important — and more often neglected — is the teaching process. Academic tradition tends to stress content while ignoring both the "how" of mental operations and the "how" of classroom interaction patterns. It seems to be assumed that mental operations are the student's private responsibility and that classroom interaction patterns are covered by the rituals of lecture, lab, and recitation. We stress that what goes on in a section should be direct practice for what will be expected later on in tests or in papers. If, for example, the test will ask students to make complex judgments concerning historical forces, there should be plenty of integrative, analytic discussion in class. If the test is to be based on multiple-choice or short-identification questions, however, it is quixotic to expect students to get interested in broad issues; it is better to help them with the mnemonic skills necessary to keep facts and dates in their heads.

The latter point provides a lead-in to handling Box 5: orienting students to course expectations. Some TAs fear answering students' questions about testing, because they do not want to "give away" the exam. I sometimes point out that this reluctance leads to an equally untenable stance: "Let's confuse students as much as possible about how they are going to be tested so that they will not study for the test, but will learn a lot of material so as to be prepared for anything." This stance is neither fair nor efficient. What is the alternative? We return again to the governing role that well-formulated objectives can play in teaching. If the objectives are broadly described and involve intellectual challenge, and if that challenge is embodied in the measurement/grading system, then both the content and the thinking approach required can be conveyed to students via syllabi, assignments, and class activities. If assignments and activities are similar to graded performances that will come later, and if this parallel is made clear to students, then they can be led to adopt a useful mental set without the teacher's giving away specific bits of test information.

Learning Format Designs

The most exciting and creative aspect of teaching may well involve filling in Box 4: devising a learning process. Here lies the challenge to arrange class interaction so as to stimulate various sorts of thinking, communicating, and learning in pursuit of specified outcome objectives. As mentioned earlier, the "how" of teaching is at once the most pivotal and the most neglected aspect of course design, especially in higher education: pivotal, because it simultaneously orients students to what is expected and embodies ultimate objectives in concrete form; and neglected, because of the pervasive tendency to think of learning only in terms of content and to take for granted the standard formats of lecture, lab, and recitation. For these reasons, the remainder of this chapter provides practical ways by which TAs can enhance learning by consciously developing the "hows" of classroom process.

Drawing Out Student Questions. Figure 1 is borrowed from our program's teaching newsletter, and is aimed at focussing TAs' attention on the subtle barriers that can prevent student participation.

Of course, the final conclusion in Figure 1 may be perfectly correct, but it may also be the result of subtle communication barriers. In Figure 1, these include the facts that there is no clearly defined way for the individual student to respond and that there are only very narrow ways in which everybody can respond (simultaneous head nods or shakes). Then, too, the instructor's question implies that he or she is poised to continue and only needs the class's assent, and so anyone raising a question must swim against this current. Finally, any student who does ask a question is labeled as one who is slow to get the point. For all these reasons, many students who do have important questions will be reluctant to speak up.

What, then, to do? We find that some deceptively simple changes can improve students' responses and help instructors read the level and direction of students' concerns. Consider this alternative to the first question in Figure 1: "Who would like me to discuss this some more?" (This question is accompanied by a gesture indicating that students should raise their hands if they do want more explanation.) This formulation has many advantages. It provides indi-

Figure 1. Unraveling the Mysteries of Classroom Communication

After years of work, we have finally cracked the nearly impenetrable code of educational communication. This breakthrough is based on the realization that the quickest way to misunderstand a message is to assume that it means what it says. Here, we offer one sample from our *Dictionary of True Educational Meanings*.

"Finding Out How Much the Students Understand"

What the instructor says:

"Does everybody understand this?"

What the instructor apparently means (and may sincerely intend):

"Would anyone who doesn't understand please indicate this by asking a question so that I can explain further?"

What the students hear:

"I hope you understand this, but if you don't, I don't really have time to explain it to you, because I have a lot to cover and I have to keep moving to hold the interest of the people who do. Besides, you dummy, you should be prepared so that you will understand, and if you can't, maybe you don't belong here, so for God's sake, if you don't understand, don't bother me about it, and try to look as if you do understand."

What the students do:

Nothing.

What the instructor concludes:

"These people aren't interested. They just want to sit there like bumps on a log and have me pour stuff into their minds without their having to think."

vidual students with a clearly defined mode of responding. It creates a channel for group responses, which can be pooled to give the instructor an overview of class understanding. It enables students to respond simultaneously and thus avoids singling out any individual. It indicates a genuine readiness to stop and explain further. And it provides a face-saving label: Wanting more discussion carries less of a stigma than not understanding. As a result, the psychological threshold to participation is lowered.

Agenda Setting. This format elaborates on the example in Figure 1 by establishing a new system for handling puzzlements. Jointly with the students, the instructor sets an agenda at the start of each session. An agenda is so familiar that we take it for granted in most formal meetings; its lack in a classroom is seldom noticed, and the result is considerable confusion and inefficiency. *Agenda* means a list on the board (to which all present can contribute) of the most important topics to be covered in a TA-led section. The TA asks, "What topics or questions are on your minds — interesting or perhaps confusing questions that we should cover today?" The TA then acts as recorder or clarifier as ideas are brought up. Often students spark each other's thinking and remind each other of missed points. The TA, too, may add items if he or she is aware of important topics that students have not mentioned. Another function of the TA is encouraging additions to the list, which ensures that all students take the risk of speaking up. If the list is too long or diverse, a show of hands can determine the priorities of the class as a whole, and some items can be deferred to office hours.

What are the advantages of agenda setting? The most obvious is that it gives everyone a clear roadmap of what the class session will deal with and thus, paradoxically, gives more control both to the TA and to the students: to the TA, because he or she can see the whole spectrum of student concerns and anticipate how to handle them; and to the students, because they have a clear channel for getting their needs met and can also anticipate what will be covered in the rest of the session. By contrast, when the TA simply asks if there any questions, everyone is left in the dark: How many other students have this question? What other sorts of questions are not being asked? What is most important? These uncertainties are removed by an agenda. Also, the TA can more gracefully handle a question to which he or she does not know the answer by deferring it or by using the time it takes to complete the agenda to search his or her memory for the answer. Finally, the TA can also reshape and integrate the list — for example, by combining several initially unrelated items into a single topic that can be handled in a unitary way.

From the student side, contributing to an agenda is an opportunity to get one's concerns raised. The TA continues adding to the list until even the most reluctant students will have had their chance. And, once one's item is securely on the list, one can relax and really pay attention to all the other answers. Finally, the fear of not asking a "good" question is reduced. One can simply indicate a topic in one or two words, without feeling pressure to articulate confusion cleverly.

Icebreakers. Icebreakers are simple, light ways of warming up the class so as to maximize personal contact in teaching. The problem with many icebreakers is that they are often seen by college teachers as frivolous or time-consuming or both. Two simple ones, which largely avoid these drawbacks, are (1) brief pair discussion and (2) milling and matching.

In brief pair discussion, the TA says, "Please turn to the person next to you, introduce yourselves, and talk for two minutes." The TA can assign almost any topic to be discussed. The discussion can be about confusion left from last week's lecture, and resulting questions can be fed into an agenda, or it can be about a key question that introduces the day's topic. It can also be about the next steps to take in solving a complex science problem or about one's opinion on a controversial issue. In any case, this is a relaxed way to foster acquaintance and also get almost everyone in the class talking and thinking actively in a short amount of time.

Milling and matching involves "milling" — free circulation of students, in which brief one-to-one contacts are made. Each student has been given a bit of information, and attempts to find one or more others with matching or related bits. Since each temporary pair must discuss their respective pieces of information, there is opportunity for lots of introductory contact and a chance to review some aspect of course material. For example, a chemistry TA gave each student a diagram of a complex molecule and asked successive pairs to discuss whether their two molecules would bond together or not. A literature TA gave out short passages from several works under study, and asked students to judge, on stylistic grounds, whether each partner's passage was written by the same author. For a review session, a sociology TA gave half the students the names of key concepts, while the other half had brief descriptions of social behavior; the task was for each pair to decide whether one partner's behavior sample was an instance of the other's concept. Milling and matching requires more time than agenda setting—about ten to fifteen minutes—but it has the same basic virtue of being time-efficient and combining acquaintance-ship with informal learning.

Student-Formulated Questions. Formulating a good discussion question is an excellent way to crystallize one's own understanding of material. As a means of encouraging students to think actively, TAs have found it useful to give them the responsibility of developing questions. One TA phrased the assignment this way: "Read this poem and think about what puzzles you about it that would also be a good discussion question. Then you will ask your question and be teacher to the class." She asked students to meet in small groups for five minutes at the start to plan questions and then devoted the discussion to each group's question in turn. After a few weeks of practice, students usually produce quite sophisticated and stimulating questions—better, in fact, than those of many teachers. Another approach is to have students produce written questions as assignments. The TA selects the best ones as discussion starters and returns all questions with comments. This method can be used in science classes; for example, one chemistry TA asked his students to work in small groups and make up questions for the following week's quiz. Each group was given a key concept and asked to devise a problem exemplifying it.

Active Student Participation in Class Work. Students can take over a great deal of the learning activity in class if the format encourages them. The TA shifts from being primarily an information giver to being a guide who asks challenging questions, gives information as needed, and keeps the students on track.

One useful approach is to construct an agenda, as previously discussed. Then students form into small groups, and each group is assigned one of the major agenda items to work on. Later, each group presents its material to the entire class. Usually the mix of expertise in each small group is enough to produce an answer; if not, the TA provides suggestions and presents a summary at the end to take care of unanswered questions. In another variation, each small group is given a teacher-designated problem or question to work on; this is selected to highlight important conceptual issues. About halfway through the class session, each group nominates a spokesperson to present its solutions to the class. In one experimental research study (Andrews, 1981) this student-centered format was compared with the more usual instructor-centered style of handling chemistry sections. Students in the two types of sections did about equally well on major exams, and reported learning about the same amount from the TA, but they learned more from fellow students in the experimental format. Also, students who labeled themselves as collaborative on a question-naire learned the most from the group format, whereas the self-defined competitive students did better with the instructor-centered approach. This suggests that one must weigh student learning styles as well as teaching considerations in selecting a format.

Other TAs have experimented with the discovery method, in which students are given a minimum amount of information and asked to develop ideas creatively on their own. An intriguing example was reported in the press recently:

> Students at the prestigious Massachusetts Institute of Technology are getting credit for playing in a sandbox. In M.I.T. professor Woodie Flowers' annual design competition, students are given a package of eighty motors, gears, springs, tubes and widgets to build a machine that will move tennis balls from one end of a sandbox to the other. The winner was sophomore Mark Schlueter. His device has mechanical arms, fires a projectile at an opponent's machine to slow it down, and grasps five balls at once to carry them across an eight-foot sandbox. "They hand us a pile of junk and that's what we have to use!" Schlueter said. "What they teach us in this class is that nothing works the first time."

In the natural sciences, a systematic approach to discover learning based on the work of psychologist Jean Piaget has been developed by Karplus (Karplus and others, 1977). Using this method, we recently conducted a comparative study of discovery and lecture-demonstration teaching as part of a TA-led pre-midterm review session in chemistry. The lecture group was given a presentation on stereoisomers (variations in the structure of molecules) followed by an opportunity to demonstrate the main points by using small kits from which molecule models could be assembled. The discovery group was simply given a brief definition of *stereoisomer* (which they had already heard about in lecture and read about in their textbook) and then given various tasks (some using the molecule model kits) to be accomplished in small groups, with the TA acting as a consultant. Unlike the M.I.T. contest, this was a routine teaching task, conducted under the usual pre-examination pressures and tensions.

We found that on a postsession quiz, the discovery students scored almost half again as high as the lecture students—9.2 versus 6.7, even though the time allotted was the same for both. There were also differences among students with different learning styles: Self-described independents liked the discovery method, while self-defined dependents were less enthusiastic. It is surprising and interesting that, in spite of these differences in attitude, both types of students did better in the discovery format; the difference is only in the size of the advantage. For the independent students, the gap was very large (10.4 versus 6.5) while for the dependent students, it was only 8.7 versus 7.0. This is strong evidence that the less structured discovery methods have a useful place in the daily activities of most undergraduate courses, even in the "one-answer" sciences, and that they are a valuable option for TAs to consider. Besides, they're fun!

We have also found it useful to base TA-led discovery activities on the brainstorming method (Osborne, 1963). This approach enhances divergent thinking by dividing problem solving into two phases. In the first phase, participants are encouraged to generate as many ideas as possible, deliberately suspending their doubts and criticisms. Apparently wild ideas are encouraged, while evaluation and disagreement are prohibited. This phase generates an uninterrupted flow of ideas, which are recorded. Then, in the second phase, the group sets up evaluative criteria; weighs, combines, and elaborates ideas; and eventually moves toward selecting those that are most useful.

For example, one literature TA began a discussion of Hemingway's *A Farewell to Arms* with this question: "What possibility for refuge are there in this novel?" He listed a variety of student suggestions on the board, adding others of his own; some provocative ideas began to emerge. One student suggested "Death might be a refuge from the fear of death," while another said, "This may sound strange, but everyone seems to be eating all the time in the book!" Later, the group examined these and many other forms of refuge, tested their ideas against textual evidence, and began to develop their own interpretation of the novel.

The natural sciences, too, are amenable to the brainstorming approach, even though conventional campus wisdom has it that these are disciplines in which creativity is possible only after years of absorbing information. Certainly, the M.I.T. project cited above would have been aided by brainstorming; and, on a more basic level, there are many times when multiple-answer group activities are very helpful. In solving mathematical word problems, for example, a first task is to extract from the problem statement the givens and other relevant data. The TA could say, "Let's list on the board all the information we can get from this problem." Later, at a difficult point in the problem solution, the TA could list various concepts, formulas, and approaches students think will be helpful, just as was done with the "refuge" example.

Brainstorming rearranges the classroom in several advantageous ways. In the first phase, it helps students feel free to participate by removing the fear of being judged wrong or looking foolish, since evaluative comments are temporarily out of bounds. Later, when the ideas are evaluated, they are somewhat detached from the person who voiced them, since they are included in a list; hence, the situation is safer, and students are also encouraged to support each other, since one person's idea often will suggest a related idea to someone else. Finally, brainstorming helps students develop, through its two phases, the intellectual skills of synthesis and evaluation (Bloom, 1956).

Debates create another dynamic that is the polar opposite of brainstorming. While brainstorming favors collaboration, debates sharpen conflict and subject ideas to challenge and testing. For certain purposes, debate can be very useful. In one debate variant, called the change-your-mind debate, the room is divided into three banks of chairs: one for each of the two opposing sides, as is customary in debates, and a third bank for the undecided. As the debate proceeds, the key ground rule is that any time a person changes his or her mind—from one side to another, from undecided to decided, or vice versa— he or she is to get up and move to the area of the room that represents his or her new viewpoint. This movement provides a fluidity missing in typical debates and leads people to evaluate their ideas continually instead of rigidifying them. It also means that the spatial arrangement of the participants is at any one moment a "snapshot" of how the debate is going; even those not speaking are making statements through their seating positions. The philosophy TA who invented this format believed it would lead to his main teaching objective: to help students develop philosophical argumentation skills.

Another way in which students can take responsibility is by devising the debate question. Sometimes the question is selected by brainstorming and then choosing one that is certain to stir up issues crucial to the class. For example, one ecology-minded group in a wilderness policy course chose to debate whether Eskimos should be restricted in their killing of seals. They realized that their general values supported both the preservation of the Eskimos' traditional way of life (which depended on a seal-slaughtering economy) and the protection of an endangered species. Pitting these values against each other was sure to produce a searching examination of how they should be applied. The debate format can also be used in "one-answer" disciplines if the issue is carefully chosen. For example, a TA in one fluid-mechanics lab posed a problem to his students that was based on an application of Toricelli's law. This TA had learned by experience that students tended to be polarized in their intuitive solutions to this problem, which provided the makings of a fruitful change-your-mind debate. The students were able to use the debate format to work out and support their solutions to the problem on general conceptual or precise mathematical grounds.

Learning Objectives–Based Review Sessions. Here, we return to the theme of objectives. TAs should plan their section activities with learning outcomes in mind, and students will learn best if they have a "roadmap" based on those objectives. Thus, the same five-step framework by which TAs and professors can orient themselves should also be helpful to students.

One literature TA conducts an objectives-based review near the end of the term. It is organized around a series of three short brainstorming activities, which conclude by preparing students to handle the essay exam. The first segment deals with the broad skills that students felt they were expected to learn, or did learn, from the course. In an English literature class, for example, students contributed such objectives as "learning to love Chaucer," "relating the author's message to the time," "seeing how humans viewed the world," "tying together universal themes," "understanding how to analyze a work of literature." The TA selected the last two of these for emphasis and conducted a second brainstorming session to compile specific themes that had arisen during the course: ambition versus desire, the individual versus the supernatural, concepts of time, and issues of the family, for example. Finally, the TA chose one of these themes, which she knew would not be on the exam, and worked through a sample essay-construction sequence with the students. Three columns were drawn on the board. The first listed works in which some aspect of the theme had appeared, the second listed the aspect of the theme at issue in each work, and the third dealt with more specific situations in which these aspects arose. The students were then asked to choose the three works that they found to be the most similar and to develop thesis ideas and topic sentences for an essay, as they would on the exam. These ideas and topics were shared with the class, and the similarities and differences among them helped students refine their conceptions of what could be done with the assignment. Thus, they were given new tools for planning an on-the-spot exam essay and were also helped to see the assignment in the context of course objectives.

Another and somewhat simpler review was carried out in a history class. The TA began by asking, "What kinds of questions do we need to answer on the topic of slavery? What are the main points you would expect to handle on the short-essay exam?" Without commenting, except to stress conceptual rather than "facts and dates" questions, she gathered a brainstorm list from students. Then she began eliciting answers from the class, guiding them with leading questions extrapolated from the list. In the end, the students answered most of the questions and they also benefited from defining the conceptual scope of the topic for themselves.

Similar things can be done in the natural sciences. Asking students in small groups to construct quiz problems is one approach; by working out how each conceptual area can be represented by a problem at an appropriate level of difficulty, students learn much about the needed skills. A related method is to conduct a problem-solving skills brainstorm, in which students list all the tricks, tips, strategies, and general rules that usually characterize problem solvers. In teaching workshops, we often ask TAs to provide the same kind of list. They have come up with fascinating examples: "There may be unneeded information—learn to select what's relevant"; "Define the goal—what the solution will look like—and work backward"; "When you've worked out a solution procedure, try it first on a similar but simpler problem to which you know the answer"; "Keep a notebook of problems you found difficult; use it to pinpoint your charactaeristic problem-solving weaknesses."

Science TAs—most of them good problem-solvers themselves—always come up with interesting suggestions, but it takes some work: One can observe how a group struggles to articulate the intuitively developed problem-solving methods that are used habitually and often unconsciously. We point out that to convey these methods to students, one must already have them explicitly accessible and that a similar brainstorm could set off the same reflection in undergraduates or at least make them more receptive to a list subsequently provided by the TA. Again, the point is to help students develop the broad intellectual skills that distinguish an active thinker from a passive learner.

A final format, useful for dealing with tests and objectives, is called the "old exam" technique and was created by a mathematics TA on our campus. He describes it as follows:

> I bring in a collection of problems they haven't seen, including many problems chosen from old exams. These I write across the top of the blackboard. When people come in, they know they are to begin working on them. I put stars by questions from old tests. Then I field homework questions for fifteen to thirty minutes, after which we'll go over the problems I've put up. The fact that the problems are from old exams is important enough to them that they are entirely in agreement with this approach. I pick and choose among the problems, in order to have a collection which covers the conceptual problems of the current material. I usually include one or two hard conceptual problems, to keep the interest of the best students. The collection as a whole gives everyone something to do while I'm answering questions about homework that gave certain people no difficulty. And so this is purpose number two: keeping the interest of advanced students. A third purpose is giving immediate feedback. Since most midterms are fifty minutes in length, some people like to see if, before the hour is through, they can do all the questions I've put up. This gets the group actively involved in problem solving during the section, getting stuck (perhaps), and then seeing how it is done right away. Thus, a fourth purpose is to give students a realistic view of potential test material — something they're always interested in and have a right to see.

New Teaching Roles

To implement these new formats with success involves learning new conceptions of the teaching role, as well as new interpersonal skills. To help them use these formats successfully, we must lead TAs beyond the oversimplifications that many teachers begin with: at one extreme, a lecture in which all the structure is provided by the instructor; and, at the other, an open seminar, which can become, at worst, directionless.

The TA must above all educate, in the literal sense of the term, which means "to draw out." One needs a repertoire of skills — asking leading questions, paraphrasing students' comments, probing for implicit assumptions, gently turning a question around to elicit more of a student's effort, synthesizing a wandering discussion, and so on. The main trick, of course, is to provide just the right amount of guidance, so that the students neither flounder on their own nor become too dependent, but grow in mastery and confidence.

The TA needs to be a designer of learning environments; this is the idea that underlies all the varied formats presented in this chapter. The TA arranges interaction so that certain types of thinking and communicating will take place. Thus, his or her primary responsibility shifts from presentation of content to guiding the learning process. Planning skills — a sense of what will work with a given group of students to reach a given objective — are required, as well as group-management skills. TAs must know how to present an unfamiliar format firmly and clearly to students; be able to intervene to keep a procedure on track without being heavyhanded or rigid; understand when and how to modify a procedure on the spot when the situation suggests a change of direction; and be able to draw explicit learnings from such open-ended activities as discovery sessions by playing the part of recorder/synthesizer for the group. A complete training program not only should familiarize TAs with new and useful formats but also must help them develop the skills needed to implement these formats constructively.

The three functions that TAs must perform constitute the distinctive contribution that TAs can make to undergraduate education. The objective-based planning model and a repertoire of class formats are means through which TAs can implement those functions. Much of the challenge in being a TA comes from artfully blending these functions, sometimes divergent or even contradictory in actual practice, into a working whole.

There is one more potential benefit in using the array of techniques described in this chapter, but this benefit will emerge only if they are used widely and frequently. Imagine that students, in moving from class to class, experience not only a variety of subject matters and ideas, but also a variety of formats for thinking and communicating. As Perry (1968) points out, the continued clash of ideas in college gradually shakes loose the preconceptions with which an entering freshman begins, but usually the medium for transmitting these ideas is limited and taken for granted. There are lectures, labs, and recitation sections; but suppose, instead, that the range of formats were as fresh, as interesting, and as diverse as the ideas themselves? Imagine a student saying, "I go from a class where we do debates right into a class where we work together on a group project. In the next class, we make up test questions for each other. It really gets me thinking!" Students in such a setting could begin to get the idea that different group formats are good for different kinds of thinking and communicating and in fact often shape thinking and that it is better to choose formats purposefully than simply to fall into them. This awareness would be a valuable contribution to any student's liberal education.

62

References

Andrews, J. D. W. "Teaching Format and Student Style: Their Interactive Effects on Learning." *Research in Higher Education,* 1981, *14,* 161–178.
Bloom, B. S. *Taxonomy of Educational Objectives.* New York: Longmans Green, 1956.
Karplus, R., Lawson, A. E., Wollman, W., Appel, M., Bernoff, R., Howe, A., Rusch, J. J., and Sullivan, F. *Science Teaching and the Development of Reasoning.* Berkeley, Calif.: Regents of the University of California, 1977.
Mager, R. F. *Preparing Instructional Objectives.* Belmont, Calif.: 1975.
Osborne, A. F. *Applied Imagination.* New York: Scribner's, 1963.
Perry, W. G., Jr. *Forms of Intellectual and Ethical Development in the College Years: A Scheme.* New York: Holt, Rinehart & Winston, 1968.
Polya, G. *How to Solve It.* Princeton, N.J.: Princeton University Press, 1973.
Whimbey, A., and Lochhead, J. *Problem Solving and Comprehension.* Philadelphia, Pa.: Franklin Institute Press, 1980.

*John D. W. Andrews is director of teaching development programs
at the University of California, San Diego. He is also a clinical
psychologist with Student Psychological Services.*

The use of an increasing number of foreign TAs now complicates
the use and development of TAs themselves. The problem calls
for more than a quick "language fix."

Rethinking the "Foreign TA Problem"

Michele Fisher

The late 1940s and the early 1950s saw the establishment of the TA as a permanent member of undergraduate instruction teams at American research-oriented universities. The 1960s and the 1970s witnessed the proliferation of training programs for these TAs. The 1980s seem to be the decade of a new TA challenge: the foreign or non-native speaking TA.

For some universities, this challenge is already several years old. A few have responded with special, usually voluntary, screening and training programs. Others have not only failed to face the problem but also have abandoned promising remedies. In either case, universities overwhelmingly are treating the "foreign TA problem" in isolation rather than in the context of general policies concerning foreign students, on the one hand, and TAs, on the other. Until such general policies are adopted, unfair and costly burdens will continue to be placed on foreign TAs, a group already struggling to adjust to an alien and demanding environment. For as long as this situation persists, the same burdens will also fall on universities themselves.

The Problem

Why is there a sudden concern about foreign TAs? And—more ominously—why do they now seem to represent a problem that needs to be addressed? The issue of foreign TAs is only one result of a significant shift in the demographics of foreign and native graduate students in the United

J. D. W. Andrews (Ed.). *Strengthening the Teaching Assistant Faculty.* New Directions for Teaching and Learning, no. 22. San Francisco: Jossey-Bass, June 1985.

States. Foreign graduate students not only are continuing to come to American campuses in large numbers but also have become vital to certain institutions and to whole fields of advanced study (Goodwin and Nacht, 1983). As a result, foreign graduate students, who are often most numerous in the very fields American undergraduates are now flocking to, have had to be thrust into the TA role in great numbers. The difficulties that were avoided for years by assigning foreign students to research assistantships or grading must now be faced. Thus, on campus after campus, there have been loud complaints from undergraduates about the language and teaching skills of foreign TAs (Bailey, 1982b; Beukenkamp, 1981; Hinofotis and Bailey, 1980; Mestenhauser, 1980; Smith, 1982).

In response, many universities have found themselves scrambling to ensure what the graduate admissions process has never pretended to address — that foreign students who are admitted, and who may later be assigned to teach, speak English adequately to perform the task. Given the pressing nature of the problem, it is hardly surprising that universities have been responding mainly with remedies that attempt to "fix" foreign TAs who are already here. Important as screening and retraining remedies are and may remain, however, they should not preclude attention to the larger issue: the need for each institution to develop a general policy on foreign graduate students.

Long-Term Solutions

A long-term policy of this kind must begin with re-examining the institution's educational, research, and community goals, as well as the part that foreign graduate students play in the realization of these goals. Then, very practical considerations must be weighed: How many foreign students can different parts of the university absorb and provide financial aid and other services for? What should these latter services be? What do they cost? Do these costs place additional burdens on the institution? Should this be reflected in differential tuition rates? Should absolute numbers of foreign students be allowed to continue rising? What about proportions within various departments and schools? There are dangers to such institutional self-study. It may oversimplify a complex problem or run the danger of arousing ethnocentric prejudices. Nevertheless, Goodwin and Nacht (1983) argue that despite such risks, the benefits far outweigh the costs; failure to come to grips with the issue may be far more risky.

Institutional self-study has another result essential to any real solution of this problem: It fosters the identification, coordination, and mobilization of staff and administrators concerned with foreign students. As it is now, Goodwin and Nacht found, high-level administrators who must make decisions concerning foreign students rarely place a high priority on the issue. Moreover, staff who are the most knowledgeable — usually foreign-student advisers — rarely have the power to shape decisions or coordinate resources. All those who can contribute should be drawn into the decision-making process. Thus, in short, if immediate solutions are not to become costly and permanent burdens, then institutions must initiate the self-studies necessary to establish financial and staff commitments to foreign graduate students.

Programs for Screening and Training

Let us turn now to some of the immediately useful programs that universities may want to develop as they start bringing the problem under control and helping TAs who already are being pressed into service.

Screening. Many institutions are beginning to realize that in the long run, a smaller amount of specialized assistance will have to be provided if all foreign graduate students who may become TAs are tested early for their spoken English. Screening could even begin with the admissions process, by a requirement for all such applicants to take a Teaching of English as a Foreign Language (TOEFL) supplement, such as the Test of Spoken English (TSE). Those who fail could be rejected outright or admitted only conditionally. At the very least, foreign graduate students should be screened as soon as they arrive on campus, and their English should be diagnosed for areas of weakness. Prospective TAs could then be tracked immediately into already existing English for Foreign Students (EFS) courses or tutoring programs. This kind of early action seems all the more advisable for the high percentage of Asian students among the TAs. Not only do Asian students report very little pronunciation work in their home-country study of English, but they also exhibit accent patterns that some American undergraduates seem to find particularly difficult (Hinofotis and Bailey, 1980, p. 128; Sarkisian, 1983, p. 6). Since improvement in pronunciation is a very slow process, screening will not guarantee flawless English, but it will give prospective foreign TAs the maximum amount of time to work on their language intelligibility, at no extraordinary expense to themselves or to their institutions.

One problem with an early screening program is that, unfortunately, no one accepted and established test of English is a sure indicator of success as a TA in the classroom. Bailey (1983b, pp. 33–35) has pointed out that it will be very difficult and complex to develop a test that can capture the spontaneous, interactive quality of the language used in teaching. Until such a test is developed, however, use of the TSE, or of some variant developed on campus, seems vastly preferable to letting foreign TAs wait until the last minute to prepare for their responsibilities.

Of course, a screening program will be effective only if the recommendations from the screening are enforced. The major adviser, who probably is in the best position to double-check a foreign student's course of study, may well share the student's resentment of the additional burden that EFS coursework represents and may allow a student to delay or neglect the coursework. The university's self-study eventually should decide who will coordinate foreign-student services and therefore follow up the screening. Until that decision is made, the graduate dean's office may need to take on this responsibility.

Training Programs. A screening program can make the problem of foreign TAs more manageable by eliminating those with serious problems and seeing that those who need some help get it through existing channels. In the short run, however, such a program does little for foreign students who are already on campus and may need immediate preparation to teach. Even in the long run, screening will not be enough for the foreign TA who has learned very good English but knows too little about the culture of the American classroom or the psychology of the American undergraduate. In the latter two situations, universities may want to adopt a variety of training programs — orientations, workshops, or courses on teaching. Some of these activities may be as brief as a day, and others may last for a semester or even longer.

The format a university chooses will probably depend on its financial and personnel resources, but it also should depend on a closer look at the specific problems its TAs are having in the classroom. These could be determined by student questionnaires, selective classroom observation, interviews, and so on. Fortunately, a very useful study has been done at UCLA and was based on observation as well as on student evaluations (Bailey, 1982b). The results of this study indicate that, beyond a certain minimal competency in English, the success of foreign TAs depends most on their ability to facilitate classroom interaction with their students. The five following areas seem particularly crucial: knowledge of American rules of conversation and discourse management; use of such re-enforcing nonverbal behaviors as eye contact and hand gestures; flexibility and appropriateness in such informal speech acts as greeting and leavetaking; ability to combine commentary with boardwork, rather than having to separate speaking from writing; and effective receptive skills, such an understanding and replying to students' questions (Bailey, 1982b, pp. 153–165).

If other campuses discover that their foreign TAs need work along similar lines, then short-term training, while still useful for other purposes, hardly seems sufficient for learning the repertoire of behaviors under question. A whole course, with the opportunity to learn the necessary behaviors under close observation over as long as three months, seems the most desirable kind of program and already exists at many leading research-oriented universities, thirteen of which report semester- or quarter-long courses (Bailey, Pialorsi, and Zukowski-Faust, 1984, pp. 43–50).

What do such courses look like? For those courses reported in other literature thus far (Cake and Menasche, 1982; Franck and DeSousa, 1980; Hinofotis and Bailey, 1980; Landa and Perry, 1980; Mestenhauser and others, 1980; Parsons and Szelagowski, 1983; Sadow and Maxwell, 1982; Sarkisian, 1983) the answers vary, but strongly similar elements also emerge, as discussed below.

Performance Component. In most courses, students give presentations as often as once a week. These are audiotaped or videotaped and critiqued by teachers (and often, according to established guidelines, by fellow students).

Some programs are even able to arrange for undergraduates to be an occasional audience (Franck and DeSousa, 1980, p. 5). Ideally, the presentation is varied enough to include practice in lectures, discussions, reviews, and introductions to lab work. Whenever appropriate, prospective TAs are encouraged to achieve significant student participation. The presentations are frequently followed by question-and-answer periods, so that TAs can also work regularly on their receptive skills.

Lectures, Tapes, and Demonstrations of Teaching Skills. These give the course participants tips on preparing and delivering material and provide the opportunity to see examples of what is considered effective teaching by American standards.

Culture of the American Classroom. Prospective TAs are given information on various aspects of American campus life: norms of politeness; teacher/student expectations and roles; and guidelines on local customs or rules that concern grading exams, holding office hours, counseling students, working with faculty, and balancing coursework with teaching responsibilities. TAs seem to benefit especially from role playing, enacting typical or difficult interactions with students and then discussing the results. Role playing reveals the often considerable gulf between foreign TAs' expectations of student responsibilities and undergraduates' notions of their own rights.

Language Practice. Most courses contain sessions on pronunciation improvement, stress, intonation, and the vocabulary of teaching. As much as possible, however, since problems of accent and stress are idiosyncratic, help in these areas is provided on an individual basis. Students are encouraged to work on their own particular problems through work in the language laboratory or with a tape recorder. Exercises in the vocabulary of teaching seem a better use of in-class time, since most students need to increase their precision and flexibility.

Above all, the course must prepare foreign TAs to make a transition more difficult than the one native-speaking TAs must undertake when they move from being learners to being teachers. The foreign TA not only has to face all the typical challenges but also must worry about how students will react to the language problem, whether to say anything about this problem, whether it will be possible to understand and answer students' questions, how to avoid doing the wrong thing because of not yet understanding American culture, and sometimes whether exasperation with American informality and ethnocentrism will be too evident.

Still worse, the foreign TA must learn to handle the ambiguous status and authority of the TA position. For many if not most foreign students, there are no TAs in the home-country institution; there are just powerful professors and powerless students. There is usually little classroom interaction. As TAs, suddenly foreign students have to act as intermediaries between students and professors, have to guide discussions, or have to get students to respond during reviews—all processes that they rarely may have witnessed.

To help with this transition, then, any course for foreign TAs must provide a participative, welcoming environment that the students may not know how to respond to at first but will probably grow to enjoy over time. Within this environment, moreover, issues of interaction must be frequently pointed out and discussed. Students must be allowed to express their perplexities and discomforts and to practice encouraging and responding to interaction. As mentioned, role playing can be especially helpful in getting students to act out situations that may still seem strange and intimidating.

Even then, foreign TAs should be warned that, whatever their preparation and training, the transition may not go smoothly. Undergraduates may still be slow to accept a foreign accent and "differentness." One of the most outgoing, verbal, and accomplished teachers in the foreign TA course at Stanford reported that he had trouble at first winning his students' trust and confidence. Some of his students did not bother to hide their disappointment at not having a native-speaking TA, and most held back from asking questions or coming to office hours. This TA eventually felt that he had won his students' confidence; even then, students needing help had access to himself as well as to a native-speaking TA and always went to the other. Fortunately, he did not take their preference personally. He understood that they simply had more confidence in the native speaker's ability to understand and answer their questions.

Any concrete help the course can offer foreign TAs in making their transition to teaching and dealing with undergraduates will help build confidence and contribute to success. The course can certainly help TAs try to see things from the undergraduate point of view, especially when the problem is the tremendous pressures undergraduates face to do well and their consequent discomfort with a TA whose English may not be as flexible or precise as a native's. Undergraduates can be invited to talk about their situation to the TAs, or tapes can be shown of undergraduates discussing their expectations of and experiences with TAs in general.

Beyond these steps, foreign TAs can be armed with useful strategies for the classroom. They can be encouraged to acknowledge the language problem to students and be given a chance to practice this acknowledgment until they feel comfortable with it; TAs whose acknowledgments seem too apologetic or too belligerent can be advised to try a slightly different tone. TAs can also be coached to use the blackboard and/or handouts frequently so as to minimize any language-based misunderstandings. TAs with really serious problems in fluency and vocabulary can be encouraged to set up small-group work for their students, if appropriate to the subject, so that instead of lecturing they can circulate as consultants and engage in easier types of communication. In fact, foreign TAs can be introduced to a type of interaction they are generally unused to—brainstorming—by asking them to identify their potential teaching problems as well as an array of possible solutions. The TAs will be much more likely to see the value of interaction if they have experienced its benefits for themselves.

The establishment of a foreign TA course also means, however, that possibly vexing administrative decisions on its nature must be resolved early. Should the course be voluntary or compulsory, graded or pass/fail, credit or no credit? If a university has set up the course after a general self-study of its foreign students, then such decisions — particularly those involving budget commitments — will be easier to reach. If the aim is to ensure that every foreign TA who will teach has been fully prepared to do so, then the course should be compulsory for everyone whose screening results showed serious weaknesses. While anything that is compulsory does create motivation problems, the university should be no more hesitant to require effort in this direction than it is in requiring successful completion of qualifying exams, orals, and a host of other hurdles. If the course is also offered for credit and without cost, participants will be well aware of the institution's seriousness and strongly influenced by its commitment.

The question of whether to grade the course is perhaps the trickiest. While assigning grades may seem still another important way to signal institutional seriousness, as well as to let departments know about the competency of their students who have completed the course, grades can present pitfalls. When we introduced a grading system at Stanford, we conceived it mainly as a way to help departments gauge the readiness of their students for successful teaching. An A meant that the student could be expected to teach successfully; a B, that the student might experience some problems in teaching and should probably be evaluated by the department at mid-quarter; and a C, that the student needed additional work before taking a TA assignment. At the beginning of the quarter, students were thoroughly informed about the system and its variance from the way they were probably accustomed to being graded. We found, however, that our foreign students were so used to striving for and achieving A's that, in our course, they regarded a B, not to mention a C, as a calamity. Some were frantic to perform at an A level, even though the kinds of changes required for them to deserve such a grade were major indeed. As a consequence, we reverted next quarter to a pass/fail option, with highly satisfactory results. Students continued to work hard, but to better their own performances rather than try to ensure good grades; departments wanting more information on their students' readiness to teach could simply request informal evaluations from our course's instructors. Certainly, it should also be possible to set up a system whereby departments would regularly receive written evaluations on their students' performances in the course, in addition to their pass/fail grades.

An ideal training program, then, would be centered around a compulsory, well-staffed semester- or quarter-long course on teaching. Other training formats, such as fall orientations, one-day workshops, or handbooks for foreign TAs, might also be desirable but should be seen as complementary to, not substitutes for, the comprehensive course. These other activities could cover additional areas of information or provide follow-up assistance to the TAs. At Stanford, we offer a workshop for foreign TAs as part of a general orientation for all new graduate students, but it is in no way a substitute for our quarter-long foreign TA course. Several manuals for foreign teaching assistants are listed in the references.

Thought must also be given to providing for students who do not pass the course. In many cases, a department can support a particular student only through a teaching assignment. If the student cannot be given one, then his or her entire course of study will be jeopardized. Some departments may feel that they have to make the assignment anyway. To prevent such assignments, the graduate dean (or whomever else the institution's self-study has designated to coordinate foreign student policy) should offer to negotiate with departments to provide other, temporary sources of support to the student involved. Obviously, if steps are not taken so that departments are not given such bailouts frequently, then they will have little incentive to encourage their students to take the foreign TA course seriously.

Follow-Up

Thus far, few institutions seem to have developed well-thought-out continuing or follow-up support to the graduates of foreign TA courses. At a minimum, all campuses must begin to consider tracking these graduates, so that the results of the training can be assessed and the recommendations acted on. At least one recent study discusses the fate of graduates one year to fifteen months after training (Landa and Perry, quoted in Bailey, Pialorsi, and Zukowski-Faust, 1984); many more of these kinds of studies are still needed. Institutions should also consider doing what the Harvard–Danforth Center for Teaching and Learning has done: to bring their graduates back after they have begun their first teaching assignments and ask them to discuss how their training helped and what, if anything, it did not cover (Sarkisian, 1983, pp. 1–2). Institutions may also want to incorporate a strategy we use at Stanford: A whole session of the course is devoted to ways in which foreign TAs can and should monitor their own progress by using campus resources; as a result, foreign TAs do use these resources for self-help after the course is over.

Good follow-up can also be facilitated by faculty under whom the foreign TAs will work. The TAs, for example, can attend weekly meetings with professors about courses and sections; these meetings could prove even more vital than such meetings normally would be. Professors can emphasize in advance the most important topics to be covered, giving foreign TAs more time to identify the vocabulary and territory that they will need to have under control. Professors can also make grading policies very explicit. If such matters are settled in detail beforehand, foreign TAs will feel more confident grading students and handling student complaints. They will also avoid the experience of a foreign TA at Stanford who, used to the British tutorial system, had made few written comments on his students' papers, expecting that they would come in to his office to talk. Instead, of course, the students were upset that he had written little except their grades. There were several complaints and some ill will before the TA was able to clarify his real intentions.

Faculty, especially, should re-examine the impact on foreign TAs of a laissez-faire attendance policy for sections. If students are free to choose their sections—or, indeed, whether or not they will attend—foreign TAs may find themselves with small sections or steadily dwindling ones. While this can happen to any TA, and would demoralize anyone it did happen to, it is especially dismaying for foreign TAs. They may have had to put a great deal of time into acquiring vocabulary or preparing outlines or even complete texts of their remarks. If few or no students show up, they probably will not want to take such pains in the future. A foreign TA may also find that students leave as soon as they discover that their teacher has an accent. Such defection not only makes a successful teaching experience impossible for the foreign TA but also may end up unfairly burdening native-speaking TAs.

Faculty may adopt an open-section policy in the first place, of course, because they would rather have disgruntled or anxious students find a TA whom they like than have to deal with complaints about a foreign TA. The faculty may even genuinely like and respect their foreign TAs, but feel resigned about their accents, their limited vocabularies, or any other real or imagined problems. Certainly, there is no easy way out of this dilemma, since many foreign TAs need a large time investment from others to be successful, and faculty may not have the time to give. Only a long-term policy, which tries to identify language problems early, provide relevant coursework, and offer training in how to teach, seems to be a way out. The difficulty is to convince faculty of the need for such a policy, when they are used to solving the problem in ways that are much more makeshift but often successful in the short run.

Faculty are unlikely to do anything special for their foreign TAs unless otherwise encouraged by the administration or department chairs. Faculty primarily view their foreign students as researchers, not teachers. Indeed, at many universities, foreign students are again and again identified as the best students, the most diligent researchers, and the least demanding advisees. Under such circumstances, faculty are all too often eager to wink at or gloss over any inadequacies foreign TAs demonstrate in teaching. Only persistent pressure from an interested dean, probably working through department chairs, will motivate faculty to identify foreign TAs who may have problems and see that they get the help they need.

Institutions may also want to prepare the undergraduates whom the foreign TAs will be trying to teach (Bailey, 1983a, p. 310; Bailey, 1982b, p. 167). Can these students can be encouraged to be more appreciative of cultural diversity, more patient about adjusting to accents, more tolerant of alien viewpoints? Can sessions be scheduled into class orientations to allow foreign graduate students to talk about themselves and their contributions to campus life? Can foreign graduate students also be invited to speak in dorms or to attend undergraduate gatherings and mingle with the undergraduates informally? This is an area that institutions have not explored very much. It may well be the slow route to the kind of changes necessary, but it does deserve attention.

Ultimately, however, the real issue in any follow-up program is whether foreign TAs will be subjected to continuing scrutiny once they have finished their prescribed training and been assigned to teaching. At most institutions, they will not be. (In this way, they become much like native-speaking TAs, who may also have received some training for their classroom responsibilities but who are also neither evaluated for how well they actually do nor helped if performance falls short.) Essentially, then, after all the effort by institutions to "fix" foreign TAs, they end up in the classroom with no more to reward their effectiveness or detect and remedy their weaknesses than any other TA; and that is very little indeed.

Reconceptualizing the Problem

Surely—rather than asking foreign TAs to undergo screening and training and perhaps additional tutoring (all on top of a normal graduate load), with no more stake in their eventual success in the classroom than with those who are not so burdened—institutions should reconsider their expectations of all TAs. TAs have become an important and permanent part of the instructional staff of all our larger research-oriented universities, but in most cases their teaching is not monitored or evaluated, as the faculty's instruction now must be. It is time to consider policies that will extend compulsory training to every TA; follow up in each case with midquarter, semester, and/or end-of-quarter/semester evaluations; and provide consultation or other assistance whenever such help is indicated. Such procedures will not only complete the professionalization of a large and essential class of instructors at our universities but also provide the last and most important step in a fair and lasting solution to the "foreign TA problem."

References

Athen, G. *Manual for Foreign Teaching Assistants.* Iowa City: University of Iowa, 1981.

Bailey, K. M. "The Classroom Communication Problems of Asian Teaching Assistants." In C. Ward and D. Wren (Eds.), *Selected Papers in TESOL.* Monterey, Calif.: Monterey Institute of International Studies, 1982a.

Bailey, K. M. "Teaching in a Second Language: The Communicative Competence of Non-Native Speaking Teaching Assistants." Doctoral dissertation, University of California at Los Angeles, 1982b.

Bailey, K. M. "Foreign Teaching Assistants at U.S. Universities: Problems in Interaction and Communication." *TESOL Quarterly,* 1983a, 17, 308–310.

Bailey, K. M. "If I Had Known Then What I Know Now: Performance Testing of Foreign Teaching Assistants." Presentation given at the Conference on Second Language Performance Testing, 1983b.

Bailey, K. M. and Hinofotis, F. B. "A One-Day Workshop in Oral Communication Skills." Paper presented at the National Association for Foreign Student Affairs conference, 1980

Bailey, K. M., Pialorsi, F., and Zukowski-Faust, J. *Foreign Teaching Assistants in U. S. Universities.* Washington, D. C.: National Association for Foreign Student Affairs, 1984.

Ballard, R. J., and Stansfield, C. W. "The Test of Spoken English and SPEAK: Instruments to Assess the Oral English Proficiency of Foreign Teaching Assistants." Unpublished manuscript, n. d.

Beukenkamp, E. J. "The International Teaching Assistant's Training Program 1/19–30/81 at Cornell University." Report submitted by E. J. Beukenkamp, April 13, 1981.

Brinton, D., and Gaskill, W. "A Language Skills Orientation Program for Foreign Teaching Assistants and Graduate Students." In J. Povey (Ed.), *Workpapers in Teaching English as a Second Language.* Los Angeles: University of California, 1979.

Cake, C. and Menasche, L. "Improving the Communication Skills of Foreign Teaching Assistants." Paper presented at the National Association for Foreign Student Affairs conference, Seattle, May 1982. (ERIC document ED 225 373)

Franck, M., and DeSousa, M. "The Foreign Teaching Assistant in the American University: A Course in Communication Skills." Paper presented at the Speech Communication Association convention, New York, 1980.

Goodwin, C. D., and Nacht, M. *Absence of Decision: Foreign Students in American Colleges and Universities.* New York: Institute of International Education, 1983.

Hinofotis, F. B., and Bailey, K. M. "American Undergraduates' Reactions to the Communication Skills of Foreign Teaching Assistants." In J. C. Fisher, M. A. Clarke, and J. Schachter (Eds.), *On TESOL '80, Building Bridges: Research and Practice in Teaching English as a Second Language.* Washington, D. C.: Teachers of English to Speakers of Other Languages, 1980.

Landa, M., and Perry, W. "Classroom Communication for Foreign Teaching Assistants." *NAFSA Newsletter,* 1980, *145,* 147.

Lorsch, N., Geiger, E., and Morrison, J. *TAs as Teachers: A Handbook for Teaching Assistants at UCSB.* Santa Barbara: Office of Instructional Consultation, University of California at Santa Barbara, 1982.

Mestenhauser J., and others. *Report of A Special Course for Foreign Student Teaching Assistants to Improve their Classroom Effectiveness.* Minneapolis: International Student Advisor's Office and Program in English as a Second Language, University of Minnesota, 1980.

Parsons, A. H., and Szelagowski, L. "Communication Skills for the International Teaching Associate at Ohio University." *NAFSA Newsletter,* 1983, *122,* 114–116.

Sadow, S. A., and Maxwell, M. A. "The Foreign Teaching Assistant and the Culture of the American University Class." In M. A. Clarke and J. Handscombe (Eds.), *On TESOL '82: Pacific Perspectives on Language Learning and Teaching.* Washington, D.C.: Teachers of English to Speakers of Other Languages, 1982.

Sarkisian, E. "A Report on *Teaching in English:* A Summer Course for Non-Native English-Speaking Teaching Fellows." Unpublished report of the Harvard–Danforth Center for Teaching and Learning, 1983.

Smith, R. M. "An Intensive Summer Workshop for Foreign Teaching Assistants: A Pilot Project." *TESOL Newsletter,* 1982, *16* (3), 31.

Michele Fisher is director of the Center for Teaching and Learning at Stanford University.

Organizational-change models furnish practical hints for creating effective TA development programs.

The Process of Launching a TA Development Program

John D. W. Andrews and Contributors

In this chapter, we will draw together the major themes discussed so far and suggest some processes whereby readers can begin to develop their own TA training programs. Paradoxically, we cannot know how to get started on something until we see clearly where we want to go. Chapters One through Four have shown where one may want to go. These chapters have described various endpoints, such as program design, instructional methods, TA-professor relationships, personal development of TAs, and organizational structure. Taken together, these elements constitute viable, effective programs. We are ready now to talk about how to reach those ends. Managing the growth process of effective TA programs will differ on each program and campus.

Some Principles of Change

To explore the program development process, we began by looking at our own experiences. How had we created our own programs? What had been the crucial ingredients, effective strategies, and key turning points that had produced the final results? The editor of this sourcebook interviewed each contributor about his or her experiences seeking themes that could be generalized

J. D. W. Andrews, (Ed.). *Strengthening the Teaching Assistant Faculty.* New Directions for Teaching and Learning, no. 22. San Francisco: Jossey-Bass, June 1985.

to other situations as well as borrowing from the literature on organizational change. Can the principles of organizational change help us understand our own experiences and crystallize them in a form useful to our readers? Lindquist (1978) describes four different models of what leads people or organizations to change. These are the rational planning, social interaction, human problem solving, and political models. Each model carries with it certain ideas about change strategies.

1. The rational planning model uses theory and research to develop a logically plausible change program. The initiator relies on sound evidence and the reasonableness of the innovation to produce acceptance among members of the institution. This model is probably the most compatible with the rational style and self-image of the typical academician, but it seems to be no more complete an account of actual change processes in colleges and universities than it is in more "irrational" institutions.

2. The social interaction model stresses social networks and influence processes. The change agent works through opinion leaders and reference groups, linking innovative practices to potential adopters, whose credibility will persuade others to make similar changes.

3. The human problem solving model focuses on how individuals come to feel the need and then the willingness to change. The innovator tries to help link a problem with one or more potential solutions. This approach often involves human relations consultation to help deal with psychological barriers to change.

4. The political model is based on the view that vested interests and power bases are primary motivators. To accomplish change, we need to build powerful coalitions among interest groups and obtain authoritative decisions that will be enforced by requiring people to change their attitudes and behaviors.

Lindquist (1978) stresses the importance of "linkage" among these approaches: "We must do it all" (p. 9). Effective change management involves also knowing which of these four models, or which combinations of them, to employ at any given point. This is a useful perspective to take on our own experiences, and we hope that the following examples will clarify how different change approaches can be used in launching and guiding TA development programs.

Social Interaction and Problem-Solving Models

When we look at how people, including ourselves, have developed such programs, it is plain that the social interaction and problem-solving models have been central concepts. Almost invariably, the developers of programs — those who actually built them up, not those who formally approved or oversaw them — have made intensive use of social networks, word-of-mouth referrals, personal contacts, and such informal sources of visibility as faculty gatherings.

Problem solving has been an equally important conceptual tool. Formal and informal need surveys have identified the areas of greatest concern to TAs and to departments, and programs were devised to meet those needs. On one campus, for example, questionnaires were used; another individual read hundreds of written student critiques of courses, as a way of understanding students' concerns; still another campus held a workshop where graduate students were invited to critique and help revise the draft TA handbook. All campuses have used their informal networks as a basis of assessing faculty and TA needs.

On the whole, this approach could be termed "clinical": learning to look at the world through the eyes of the potential client (TA, faculty member, or department) and initiate action accordingly. Smock (1980) puts it this way: "As a developer I felt it was incumbent on me to learn their language rather than teaching them the language of the educationist." One important aspect of this approach is that it enables the developer to tune in to the style of the campus and shape the program accordingly. For example, one of us commented that, to blend in well, her center needed to be seen as "a funny little place" that was holding informal conversations about teaching, rather than as a powerful campus unit. Another contributor, who began his program in a similarly informal and impressionistic style, received feedback from his science-oriented campus that more structure and prescriptiveness was wanted, and so his program evolved accordingly to match the campus style more closely. Then, too, many of us have found it essential to learn the "languages" of different disciplines — their attitudes, their unique teaching problems, their assumptions about learning — in order to reach them effectively.

Another "networking" function is a kind of low-key salesmanship designed to make potential clients aware of new services. In and of itself, conducting surveys can serve this function. Another particularly fruitful way of increasing visibility is to work through experienced, interested senior TAs. These "master" TAs help conduct training and also serve as contacts to spark interest among the graduate students in their departments. They are also a good source of information about needs the program can serve. Other routes to visibility include performing plainly understandable and needed services, such as designing student evaluation surveys for promotion and tenure files or helping new doctoral graduates with their job-seeking dossiers. Brochures, newsletters, and other sorts of publicity are also useful, as is helping to strengthen networks by putting people who have mutual interests in contact with each other. As one program director put it, "If they're comfortable with us as a result of these involvements, they'll come to us about their teaching, too."

Research and Development Approach

What we will call the research and development approach is another important model, but it must be introduced thoughtfully within the context of the networking and problem-solving activities just described. An important aspect of this approach involves the use of existing materials for local training. These include such resources as handbooks, structured guides for training activities, demonstration videotapes, and planned training curricula. We believe in the value of such materials; some of us are producers of them. Nevertheless, we also believe, with Lindquist (1978, p. 226), that the TA development coordinator must reconstitute them in a form that is acceptable to the local campus culture and its citizens. To do this effectively, the coordinator must be attuned to the internal frame of reference of the client.

Another important function of the research and development approach involves program evaluation, which also must be seen in the light of informal networks. As Smock puts it, "The judgments of those who interact daily with students, faculty, and teaching assistants and the informal accolades at the right social occasion almost certainly have had more impact on the growth of the Campus Teaching Program than the carefully prescribed results of research could have had" (1980, p. 10). More formal evaluations are still very important, however. On several campuses, these have been crucial to programs' credibility. Interestingly, some of the more effective formal evaluations have also involved informal networks and problem solving. In one case, for example, after the members of a funding committee conducted interviews directly with TAs who had participated in the program, the committee made improvement suggestions to the program developer. In another case, TA development professionals from other campuses were invited to review the program. In addition to providing suggestions, they helped link the local campus committee to broader national currents concerning teaching improvement. In still another instance, evaluation was conducted by a graduate student intern in the administrative office that had overall responsibility for the program. In each of these situations, the formal study not only provided evaluation but also changed communication patterns among key personnel on campus. It is our impression that evaluations with this social interaction element are more important to a program's viability than a more rigorous — but also organizationally disconnected — research project would be.

Implications of Political Power and Change

In our experience, the political model, involving the use of formal authority and/or political power, is rarely used directly by most program developers. Typically, we are not in top-level power roles. Even more important, perhaps, our aim — to create a constituency of individuals willing to try out new ideas about improvement in teaching — may be undercut by the overenthusiastic use of the political model. The political factor is always there in the background, however; often, it is most noticed through the problems its absence produces. Each of our programs, for example, has had significant support from the top, from a president, a dean, or another official who has smoothed the path, sold the idea, and/or provided financial support. We know of one instance in which a program collapsed for lack of such endorsement, and of another in which this same lack of support (more partial than total) made it necessary for TA training to be developed in an indirect way with the support of a friendly administrator (who was not the most structurally appropriate person to take this role).

Then, too, some minimal level of formal sanction was necessary to get each of our programs launched. In some cases, proposals were passed with ease by faculty committees or faculty senates; in others, there was opposition. On one campus, for example, the faculty turned down a proposal for a teaching development center, only to have the students apply for and obtain funding to start their own teaching evaluation survey. On several campuses, the shift in political power that occurred with the rise of student activism in the late 1960s and the early 1970s created significant pressure to do something about improving teaching. Often, program developers are the beneficiaries of such pressures; they are seen as persons who can help the campus deal with others' expectations.

Many of these cases seem to involve a delicate balance of legitimacy, visibility, and political maneuvering. Proposing a new program too forthrightly at an early stage often raises the strongest resistance, while bypassing the issue of legitimacy altogether means asking for trouble later on. Our experience suggests a middle-ground approach, in which enough legitimacy is obtained to get the program underway and—most important—to give the developer a clear field for using the networking and problem-solving change strategies. These activities, in turn, can gradually win over or defuse the opposition as more and more people come to see the program's value.

There is still another virtue to this middle ground. The use of institutional power can be seductive. As Lindquist (1978, p. 230) puts it, "On the surface, presidential fiat (or the fiat of outside money) seems much faster and cleaner than committees. You get what you want right away. Or do you?" We know of certain programs that seemed to be well launched in this way, but which did not make the transition to grass-roots support when the "fiat" ended. Experiences on certain of our campuses suggest that this transition must be prepared for and handled with great care. This transition, once again, involves social interaction and problem-solving strategies.

If the power of administrative fiat is to be used at all, it also is best used in a middle-ground way. Lindquist says that the solution most often used by "(effective) leaders. . . . was a combination of their own initiatives with increasing attempts to involve participants in setting their own goals. . . and involving themselves in implementation and evaluation" (p. 247). One dean's strategy was to introduce such a fairly bold change as a TA training requirement or a TA evaluation system, present it as a proposal to departments, and then back off when the expected resistance flared up. Later, departments worked on the idea, changed it in the light of their individual problems and needs, and came back with versions that showed the marks of their own thinking. Modified versions were usually adopted.

The element of ownership—the degree of personal involvement, access, and control felt by groups or individuals with a stake in the program—is also important in other situations. Ownership is an issue on which the "networking" and political models are sharply divided. Political approaches tend to restrict ownership, while strategies that exploit networks expand it (Lindquist, 1978, p. 65).

Thus, the social interaction and human problem solving models are the best ways to create this sort of ownership. The political model tends to establish power struggles and undermine informal networks. In particular, a program developer or an administrator should never get into a struggle with departments over who will "own" TA training. While many academic departments will not necessarily want to assume this burden, they also will resist its being taken over by a central agency that lacks disciplinary credentials. What works best is a partnership arrangement with many variations, such as Smock and Menges suggest in Chapter Two. Academic departments, as well as the central administrator or agency, should have easy access to money for TA training activities, perhaps through a grant fund established for this purpose.

According to Lindquist (1978, p. 66), "Those opposed to an innovation usually have sound reasons and legitimate concerns. Innovators need to sit down with the opposition and listen. Conservatives should not be forced to move until they are ready." Impatience with the "opposition"—with those who ignore teaching in favor of scholarship or who believe that teaching ability is inborn—is an occupational hazard of TA trainers. This impatience interferes markedly with the problem-solving and social interaction models. It is more compatible with the political model. The drawback is that an opposed group whose sense of ownership grows progressively weaker will sometimes engage in outright sabotage. Developing a constituency means taking into account all sorts of needs. By recognizing them as legitimate, through open communication, creative and more encompassing solutions can sometimes be found.

The Use of Committees

Political processes often can be blended with social interaction and problem-solving approaches through the use of committees. While committees can be ineffective and even obstructive, our experience shows that committees constituted in the way Lindquist (1978, p. 236) prescribes have been most effective in launching and supporting TA development programs. Lindquist's prescription is particularly important with respect to advisory committees for such programs. It includes provisions for outside consultation, review bodies, small groups, brief and immediately pertinent opinion questionnaires, indepth meetings and workshops, and shared leadership among faculty and administrators, as well as training in all these endeavors.

Summing Up the Change Process

Lindquist (1978, pp. 238–239) summarizes a change strategy that links the various models he presents and that we have discussed here. With respect to TA development programs, we also often see a distinctive cycling among these various change models. We may begin with the application of political influence and formal authority, which may involve student pressure groups, legislatures, boards of trustees, and/or campus presidents. The effect is to create an umbrella under which the social interaction and problem-solving models can then be used effectively by the program developer, so that the involvement generated by exploiting informal networks creates both a climate of support and an active clientele that enhance the program's credibility. This climate, in turn, can prepare the way for a new round of institutionalization: (political model) moves to establish training requirements or other arrangements that build the program more formally into institutional life.

It seems to us that, at certain points, each change model was the best and perhaps only approach, but not to have had all models available could have blocked progress; effective orchestration of them all was needed. While this cycle of model use has not occurred fully on all our campuses, we have seen several examples of it, and it seems in itself to be a useful model for the efforts of people initiating TA training programs.

What is needed to keep TA development programs fresh, to prevent them from becoming too institutionalized and from becoming problems instead of solutions? We think that the social interaction and problem-solving models will help ensure that those who guide such programs remain alert to new currents, both on and off campus, and be prepared to foster new aims. Identifying new needs and constructing ways to meet them is a key strength of our approach: to enhance TA development in the broadest sense, both at individual and at institutional levels.

References

Lindquist, J. *Strategies for Change.* Berkeley, Calif.: Pacific Soundings Press, 1978.
Smock, R. "The Development and Impact of the Campus Teaching Program." Paper presented at the meeting of the Network for Professional and Organizational Development in Higher Education, October 1980.

John D. W. Andrews is director of teaching development programs at the University of California, San Diego. He is also a clinical psychologist with Student Psychological Services.

This chapter contains a listing of handbooks for TAs, books on teaching, demonstration videotapes, discipline-centered materials, and TA program development manuals and handbooks.

Additional Resources

John D. W. Andrews

The resources listed here are intended to correspond to the issues raised throughout this volume. Instructional methods, training techniques, program designs, and institutional contexts are some of the topics covered by the categories described below. We have included listings of handbooks for TAs, general texts on teaching, discussions of teaching from the perspectives of specific subject disciplines, videotapes to be used in conducting training activities, guides and materials for program development work, and a discussion of program evaluation. Finally, because not all the knowledge that is needed can be conveyed through print or other media, we have listed two organizations that provide not only workshops on program development skills but also opportunities for contact with colleagues grappling with similar issues.

Handbooks for Teaching Assistants

These handbooks include teaching suggestions, guidelines for adapting to the TA role, bibliographies on teaching, discussions of administrative and financial matters, and other information. Some of the information is general, while other parts of these books are campus-specific, but even the latter material is useful in suggesting categories of information that a department may want to include in its own handbook. Copies of these handbooks, and information about costs, can be obtained by writing to the programs indicated.

J. D. W. Andrews, (Ed.). *Strengthening the Teaching Assistant Faculty.* New Directions for Teaching and Learning, no. 22. San Francisco: Jossey-Bass, June 1985.

The Graduate Assembly. *Handbook for Teaching Assistants.* Berkeley: University of California, 1975.

Teaching Resources Center. *TA Handbook.* Davis: University of California, 1974.

Teaching Assistant Development Program. *Teaching Assistance.* San Diego: University of California, 1978.

The Graduate School. *Teaching Assistants' Handbook.* Evanston, Ill.: Northwestern University, 1983.

Center for Teaching and Learning. *Teaching at Stanford. An Introductory Handbook.* Stanford, Calif.: Stanford University, 1976.

TA Training Program. *The TA at UCLA.* Los Angeles: University of California, 1974.

Teaching Assistant Resource Center. *Handbook: Classroom Teaching Skills.* Albuquerque: University of New Mexico, n. d.

Books on Teaching

These books can serve as general introductory texts for college teachers. They are also useful for TAs and new professors. Some are general introductions and include the major topic areas that make up the teaching process, while others deal with more specialized subjects, as indicated by their titles.

Axelrod, J. *The University Teacher as Artist.* San Francisco: Jossey-Bass, 1973.

Cahn, S. M. (Ed.). *Scholars Who Teach: The Art of College Teaching:* Chicago: Nelson-Hall, 1973.

Eble, K. E. *The Craft of Teaching.* San Francisco: Jossey-Bass, 1976.

Eble, K. E. *The Aims of College Teaching.* San Francisco: Jossey-Bass, 1983.

Fuhrmann, B. S., and Grasha, A. F. *A Practical Handbook for College Teachers.* Boston: Little, Brown, 1983.

Gullette, M. (Ed.). *The Art and Craft of Teaching.* Cambridge, Mass.: Harvard-Danforth Center for Teaching and Learning, 1982.

Milton, O., and Associates. *On College Teaching.* San Francisco: Jossey-Bass, 1978.

Lowman, J. *Mastering the Techniques of Teaching.* San Francisco: Jossey-Bass, 1984.

McKeachie, W. *Teaching Tips. A Guidebook for the Beginning College Teacher.* Lexington, Mass.: Heath, 1978.

Noonan, J. F. (Ed.). *Learning About Teaching.* New Directions for Higher Education, no. 4. San Francisco: Jossey-Bass, 1980.

Runkel, P., Harrison, R., and Runkel, M., (Eds.). *The Changing College Classroom.* San Francisco: Jossey-Bass, 1972.

Travers, R. M. W., and Dillon, J. *The Making of a Teacher: A Plan for Professional Self-Development.* New York: Macmillan, 1975.

Demonstration Videotapes

Videotapes can often be especially valuable as training tools because they enable TAs to view techniques that are often hard to apply from verbal presentations. Videotapes are also useful for helping to sharpen the trainee's perceptions of classroom events, including nonverbal communication, especially when "candid" tapes are used.

Center for the Teaching Professions. *College Classroom Vignettes.* Evanston, Ill.: Northwestern University.

Department of Chemistry. *Project TEACH.* Lincoln: University of Nebraska.

Office of Instructional Development, 62 Royce Hall. *Mastery Teaching Tapes.* Los Angeles: University of California.

Teaching Assistant Development Program. *Innovative Formats Demonstration Tapes.* San Diego: University of California.

Center for Teaching and Learning. *Lecturing and Discussion Tapes.* Stanford, Calif.: Stanford University. (This videotape is available for loan.)

University of Michigan Dental Educational Resources. *Project 119: "Trigger Episodes" in Teaching.* Ann Arbor, Mich.: University of Michigan. (This tape is useful for initiating discussions of teaching alternatives and role-playing activities.)

Teaching Resources Center. *Teaching Resources Center Videotape Collection.* Davis: University of California. (These are "candid" videotapes of classroom teaching by TAs in a variety of disciplines and formats.)

Discipline-Centered Materials

It is often helpful to provide new TAs with teaching materials dealing specifically with their subject areas. Academic departments that conduct their own training programs are apt to find such materials especially relevant. Those that conduct centralized or cross-disciplinary training programs will find such materials helpful for focusing on discipline-relevant issues and establishing the training's credibility with subject-matter specialists. One excellent source of discipline-relevant materials is the series (nos. 1–6 of *Change*) titled *Report on Teaching From the Editors of Change Magazine.*

There are also many discipline-centered teaching journals for higher education. Subscription information, too lengthy to list here, can be found in the Source Journal Index of the *Current Index to Journals in Education* (CIJE), available in most libraries or from Oryx Press, 2214 N. Central at Encanto, Suite 103, Phoenix, Arizona. These journals cover most of the standard academic subject areas. The Source Journal Index (found in each CIJE volume), in which journals are listed alphabetically, is also a good place to browse for additional information.

Program Development and Institutional Issues

Several chapters have stressed the importance of dealing effectively with TA training contexts in developing programs. Four resources are listed below. Lindquist's book provides an overview of these issues. Bergquist and Phillips, in their handbooks on faculty development, also discuss these issues, as well as offering many practical aids to determine the concerns of faculty and TAs. They share sample teaching evaluation forms and tips for developing programs. Blizzard, Hogan, and Roy's manual for developing TA training programs outlines specific steps to be taken and questions to be answered.

Bergquist, W. H., and Phillips, S. R. *A Handbook for Faculty Development.* (Vols. 1–3). Washington, D. C.: Council of Independent Colleges, 1975–1981. (Inquiries: One Dupont Circle, Suite 320, Washington, D. C.)

Blizzard, A. C., Hogan, R. C., and Roy, D. E. *Developing a Departmental Program for Teaching Assistants: A Manual.* Hamilton, Ontario, Canada: Instructional Development Center, McMaster University, 1981.

Lindquist, J. *Strategies for Change.* Berkeley, Calif.: Pacific Soundings Press, 1978.

Wood, L. *Sourcebook For Developing TA Training Programs.* Berkeley: Teaching and Evaluation Services, University of California, 1978.

Program Evaluation

A review of formal research efforts to evaluate TA training programs is found in: Carroll, J. G. "Effects of Training Programs for University Teaching Assistants." *Journal of Higher Education,* 1980, *51* (2), 167–183.

Workshops for Developing Interpersonal and Organizational Skills

As several of the preceding chapters suggest, successful TA development programs depend heavily on the organizational and interpersonal skills of those responsible for establishing and guiding them. One of the best investments of time and energy when starting a TA development program is attendance at a workshop that deals with such skills. Workshops are offered by:

National Training Laboratories Programs in Leadership for Educational Change, P.O. Box 9155, Rosslyn Station, Arlington, Va.

Network for Professional and Organizational Development, in conjunction with The Academy for Professional Development, 1514 Camino Verde, Walnut Creek, Calif.

Many of the authors cited here, and directors of campus programs for teaching assistants, are also available to conduct workshops.

John D. W. Andrews is director of teaching development programs at the University of California, San Diego. He is also a clinical psychologist with Student Psychological Services.

Index